Moral Re-Armament
What Is It?

BY

BASIL ENTWISTLE

AND

JOHN McCOOK ROOTS

PACE PUBLICATIONS

LOS ANGELES

170
E61m

CONTENTS

13584

PREFACE

The aim of this short book is threefold:

1. To explain the essentials of Moral Re-Armament to those who know little or nothing about it.
2. To give straightforward answers to questions frequently asked.
3. To make available some materials which document its development.

The book is written primarily for Americans and gives emphasis to Moral Re-Armament in the United States.

It is authoritative, in that it was written at the request of those responsible for MRA's program in America and in cooperation with them.

Moral Re-Armament is a large subject, with many facets and no book of this size can serve as more than a summary of what it is and what it has done. An attempt has been made, however, to cover factually the basic elements of what many responsible men regard as the most significant, timely and hopeful development of the twentieth century.

PART ONE

What Is It?

YOUNG AMERICA'S NEW IDEA

In the heart of America — on an island in the Great Lakes — something was created in the summer of 1965 which has caught the imagination of a generation of youth on every continent and fascinated their parents and grandparents.

This creation was the expression of American youth and their hunger for involvement and relevance in today's world. Walt Disney called it "the happiest, most hard hitting way of saying what America is all about." Said one of scores of Congressmen who had twice welcomed it to Washington, "This is exactly what we ought to be telling the world."

At 89 military bases it has moved 300,000 officers and men to rousing ovations. It has made an impact in Catholic masses, G.I. training, juvenile law courts, school classes, newspaper editorials. On more than 300 college campuses it has shattered apathy and sparked debate; and one hundred million Americans have responded to it on television.

Overseas, Japanese Marxist students who encountered this American phenomenon exclaimed, "If this is America, then we are for America." Young Panamanians, who had not long before torn down the Stars and Stripes, asked what part they could play with young Americans. Germany's mass circulation *Bild am Sonntag* commented, "America has sent over the Atlantic a new voice answering the false picture of a weak, arrogant, protesting American youth."

What was this creation? It was a demonstration, in music, initially by 130 American youth who felt that the time had come to speak up and sing out. They were not interested just in protesting against what was wrong, but in voicing for their generation what they were committed to see happen around the world. They sang of the hard work, sacrifice and faith which make a nation great. In original songs they expressed love of home, homeland and humanity. They backed up their convictions from the stage with their actions. They sold cars and prized possessions, gave up scholarships, emptied bank accounts, to finance themselves as they took to the road.

They received no salaries, worked long hours, accepted cheerfully rugged conditions, rigorous travel and disciplined living. And they mobilized thousands of youth who responded to their challenge.

Their production, known first as "Sing Out '65," then "Sing Out '66" and then, following their nationwide appearance on TV, "Up With People," during the next twelve months grew from one cast of 130 to three full-time companies of 600. Within sixteen months the "Sing Out" explosion through these casts had presented "Up With People" at over 300 colleges and schools; given the show at the four Service Academies and 89 military bases in the United States and overseas; traveled through Japan, Korea, Germany, Austria, Spain, Puerto Rico, Panama, Jamaica and Venezuela at the invitation of governments and national leaders.

3

The "Sing Out" explosion also produced a series of one-hour TV spectaculars which have been seen in the United States by an estimated 100 million from coast to coast, another which reached 25 million in West and East Germany and another which blanketed Japan; trained over 10,000 youth in more than 130 regional Sing Outs throughout the U.S. and Canada involving youth and adults in a community action program that is rebuilding the family life and enhancing the best traditions of the nation; inspired similar casts in fifteen other countries of Europe, Asia, Australasia and Latin America, including full-time casts in Germany and Japan which in turn were invited to visit other countries throughout their continents.

Invited by the governments of Germany, Austria and Spain for a seven-week tour in June 1966, "Up With People" set off a chain reaction among thousands of young Europeans. One of Germany's most prominent dailies, *Die Welt,* wrote about "Freedom Isn't Free," one of the songs of the show, "It could become the theme song of the western world." Chancellor Ludwig Erhard who received the cast and came to a performance in Bonn told them, "You have not only helped unite Germany and America but you have awakened the conscience of a nation to the fact that freedom isn't free. It is a very great thing you have done."

Within weeks, two traveling casts of "Sing Out Deutschland" were operating in Germany and more than 20 regional Sing Outs were giving a new purpose and direction to the youth of that nation. "Don't look back," ran one of their songs, "Learn from the past and take on the future."

When the young Germans performed in Flensburg, on the Danish border, in December 1966,

4

hundreds of Danes came across the border to see them, cheered their show and invited it to Denmark. "Here," they said, "is the Germany we can trust. This is the spirit which young Denmark needs and wants." Early in 1967, "Sing Out Deutschland" toured Switzerland and later flew to Brazil at the request of a committee of senior Brazilians.

Meantime, the seeds sown by the American Sing Out's visit to Japan and Korea had born similar fruit. The original cast had demonstrated its ability to capture the imagination of anti-American leftist students and enlist them in their bid to give the youth of the world a greater and more satisfying aim than those offered by Peking and Moscow. Starting at the heart of revolutionary student life, Waseda University, the young Americans launched a positive revolutionary movement on Tokyo campuses which produced the Japanese "Let's Go '66."

Commenting on the response among these supposedly anti-American students, Ambassador Edwin Reischauer told the cast at a reception he gave for them, "It means so much to have 130 young American emissaries in Japan at a time like this." The Japanese Prime Minister, Eisaku Sato, who attended a performance at which the American and Russian Ambassadors were also present, thanked the young Americans for "a job well done."

Congressman Clement Zablocki, Chairman of the House Foreign Affairs Sub-Committee on the Far East and Pacific told members of the cast, "When my Sub-Committee was in Asia, the Southeast Pacific and the Sub-Continent of India, I heard glowing reports of your tour in Asia. I never felt so proud to be an American in my life."

As in the United States, regional Sing Outs have sprung up in Japan and also in Korea where the young Americans gave their show by invitation of the Prime Minister to thousands of students, as well as to the leadership of the nation.

Then followed a further remarkable development. Through the "Sing Out" explosion in these two countries, young Japanese were invited for the first time to Korea, bridging the bitterness and suspicion still left from the Japanese occupation. "Let's Go '66" grew as a cast of Japanese and Koreans, and following a visit to Taiwan and Hong Kong, young Chinese joined the company. In December 1966 leaders of other Asian countries invited this Sing Out to Taipei, Manila, Bangkok and Kuala Lumpur and the main cities of Indonesia to launch in Southeast Asia a unity of heart and mind which could not merely withstand the advances of Peking, but might in due course win young Communist Chinese to a more satisfying idea.

During the late summer and fall of 1966 one of the three American full-time casts toured Eastern Canada. Here again suspicion and antagonism toward the United States evaporated as the young Americans performed in the cities and on the military bases. Regional Sing Outs sprang up in their wake across the country.

South of the border another American cast drew similar response. Invited to Puerto Rico in October, Panama in November, then to Jamaica, Venezuela and Mexico, by the time they returned to the United States at Christmas they had roused hundreds of thousands of youth of the Caribbean, Central and Latin America to a new hope for themselves and their nations. Castro's Cuba was sud-

6

denly ringed by countries in which his appeal to youth was met by a greater appeal. And further, as Foreign Minister Fernando Eleta of Panama said while thanking the American Ambassador for securing the visit of the cast, "We have seen a true unity of spirit between North and South America."

In all these countries "Sing Outs" mushroomed. In some cities like San Juan and Caracas rehearsals of the new casts were attended by one thousand at a time. A Puerto Rican student expressed the sentiment of many when he said, "Since the time I entered university five years ago we have let a negative minority group lead us, but here is the spirit we need in our island, and we intend to be the bridge that takes it from North to South America."

Pablo Casals, the celebrated cellist, was among the thousands of an older generation who responded with enthusiasm. "Everyone must support the ideas you sing about," he told the cast, and he offered them one of his favorite compositions for their show.

President Raoul Leoni of Venezuela hosted a gala performance in the garden of his official residence for the Cabinet, heads of government departments, the Armed Forces and the diplomatic corps. Afterwards he told the cast, "I wish you the greatest success in this tremendous mission. I hope that the youth of our country will grasp onto it. It was not just an excellent show. It was the intent and purpose behind it that was significant."

The youth did grasp onto it by the thousands at the Catholic University (largest crowd ever) and other colleges, in mass outdoor shows in bull rings, at the Military Academy and over nationwide television. In an editorial entitled "The New Diplomacy," Venezuela's leading newspaper *El Nacional* summed up the visit of the young Americans:

"The traditional diplomacy of the career diplomatic corps has become rigid, mechanical, cold, and often doesn't reach the people. Now a new diplomacy has sprung forth in the world. Its chancellors are groups of young people, ready for action, and hungry to find positive, tangible and peaceful solutions. One of these groups is in Caracas now under the theme of 'Up With People.' They aspire 'to change the human being first and consequently produce a change in environment.'

"They preach and practice that the moral rearmament of the individual is a need that cannot be postponed. This qualifies their actions as unquestionably revolutionary. They make their appeal through music and in verse and chorus. They sing 'Freedom Isn't Free,' and this is the theme which is the real key for the whole strategy of peace.

"The world is becoming bitter but not so much so that mankind cannot act with generosity, tolerance and understanding toward those that want to break away from the irrevocable antagonisms."

Even in far distant countries and continents to which no casts of young Americans had gone the Sing Out explosion produced its fall-out. "Harambee, Africa" (Pull Together, Africa) came into being as a result of four young Kenyans seeing "Sing Out '65" in America. This production received warm encouragement from President Kenyatta, and sparked thousands of Kenyans of every background, race and tribe to a new patriotism and unity. It also visited the Sudan and Ethiopia at government invitation and received thunderous response.

By the end of 1966 "Dynamite '66," another offspring of "Sing Out '65," was playing in Brazil with three casts for the Armed Forces, schools and colleges, and in the key industrial centers. Similarly musical productions were on the road in Britain, India and Australia, each undertaking a distinctive and strategic role in the life of these nations.

While all this was happening abroad, more than two million people in the United States had seen live performances of "Up With People." In addition some 100,000 each week were seeing performances by 150 regional Sing Out casts across the country.

In Washington, 161 Senators and Congressmen formed the inviting committee for performances in Constitution Hall just before the cast's departure for Germany in May, 1966.

The casts gave performances at all four Service Academies. After a return visit to the U.S. Military Academy at West Point, the second in nine months, Brigadier General John R. Jannarone, Dean of the Academic Board, said, "In my 17 years of association with West Point I have never seen anything that has received such a response from the cadets."

Two performances were given at the Air Force Academy, and it was proposed to make it an annual event. Midshipmen at the Naval Academy at Annapolis gave the cast a 31-minute hats-off standing ovation. Said one midshipman, "You show the thing in America worth defending."

The commander at a SAC Air Force Base wrote: "It was a performance none of us will forget. This young group does more in a two-hour demonstration to display a positive American spirit than almost anything I have witnessed."

The commanding general of a U.S. armored corps wrote: "'Up With People' is the finest entertainment we have ever had. Its real value and contribution to the moral and spiritual tone of this command were very great indeed."

A Marine corporal bound for Vietnam wrote: "On behalf of myself and fellow Marines in my unit we would like to extend our gratitude for the new idea which you have brought to us. It makes us realize that this country really does have something worth fighting for."

General Robert W. Porter, Jr., Commander-in-Chief of the U.S. Southern Command, who was host to "Up With People" in Panama, said to the cast, "If you keep your enthusiasm and great idealism, we can get the change that is required in the world through an orderly process instead of anarchy and bloody revolution."

Standing ovations became routine and audiences were as varied as the United States — senior government and diplomatic figures in Washington, Hollywood Bowl under the stars, veteran paratroopers back from Vietnam, Watts high school students shortly after the rioting, the American Medical Association's annual convention, G.I.'s on the 38th parallel in Korea, Hollywood notables at the Beverly Hilton, Harlem's controversial Public School No. 201, Pueblo Indians of the Southwest, University of California students, New York businessmen at the Waldorf Astoria. Young and old, rich and poor, civilian and military, sophisticated and simple, white, black, red and yellow.

When the sponsors made a count of letters received about "Up With People" telecasts they found ten thousand appreciative to forty negative. They had never known any comparable response to a program. In the press editorials and syndicated columns as well as headlines and stories echoed the surprise and delight the public seemed to feel at a new voice, a new direction and a new purpose among youth.

Here are a few of the comments:

Nashville Banner: "They came, they saw, they conquered . . . They came to fortify the spirit of young America . . . to stir to flame the embers of faith and a precious allegiance to historic principles."

Denver Post: "The entire audience (at the U.S. Air Force Academy) rose to its feet and cheered through eight encores that followed a stellar, two-hour performance. This new breed of young Americans had the audience electrified from the start."

Charlotte (N.C.) Observer: "It upgrades the positive, the purposeful, the kind of American demonstrator who shows millions of Chinese and Russians a new way to go."

Hollywood Citizen-News: " 'Up With People' is more than a musical staged with spirit by enthusiastic young people. It is a determined effort to steer other young people to bust open the spirit of this generation so that man can take up his greatest mission on earth."

Boston Herald: "Salt-nosed Cape Codders, always stingy with praise, were returning two and three times. There hasn't been a show on Cape Cod in years that could match this."

Greenville (S.C.) News: "This Moral Re-Armament bit — why sonofagun, those kids make sense!"

Christian Science Monitor: "This was a different type of youth, ready to lay its patriotism on the line and work with energy for 'the stuff of which this nation's made.' "

Santa Fe News: "These youngsters break into your heart instead of your store window; they set fire to your conscience instead of your home; they

11

march with a smile and a song of hope in lieu of grim, unreasoning demands and a club."

The Sing Out program, starting as a musical demonstration, has begun to give direction and impetus to every aspect of the life of a generation.

What was the magic which sparked standing ovations? What was the multiplying power which mobilized youth by the thousands? What idea had the power to turn the apathetic into enthusiasts, bring discipline to the flabby, give hope to the hopeless, unite divided families, cure dishonesty in schools, turn enemies into friends? These are frequent results of the visit of a Sing Out to a community. And what was the secret which made enthusiastic allies out of anti-Americans around the world?

Behind the Sing Out program of "Up With People" is a potent idea, simple, timely, practical, revolutionary.

It is Moral Re-Armament.

— 2 —

WHAT IS
MORAL RE-ARMAMENT?

Definitions of Moral Re-Armament are not very satisfactory. They are liable to include too much and be confusing, or too little and be one-sided. People are apt to approach MRA from the aspect in which they are most interested — its principles, its program or its people, or maybe its origins, its organization or its objectives. Each of these aspects will be described but it is only fair to add that the whole creature is unique. People confronted with Moral Re-Armament for the first time sometimes react like the Mid-Western farmer confronted by a giraffe. "I don't believe it," he said, "There's no such animal."

Here are a dozen attempts, however, from varied angles, to define the essence of Moral Re-Armament — what it stands for:

1. The man who started MRA, Frank Buchman, an American, speaking in June 1948 on the occasion of the tenth anniversary of its launching, said: "Moral Re-Armament is the good road of an ideology inspired by God upon which all can unite. Catholic, Jew or Protestant, Hindu, Muslim, Buddhist and Confucianist — all find they can change, where needed, and travel along this good road together."

2. He added in a speech one year later: "Moral

Re-Armament has the tremendous uniting power that comes from change in both East and West. It gives the full dimension of change. Economic change. Social change. National change. International change. All based on personal change.

3. The U.S. Department of Justice in an interoffice memorandum of April 1, 1949, wrote: "Moral Re-Armament is a world force having as its principal objective adequate ideological preparedness of free nations for the ideological conflicts in which the world is now engaged. Its objectives are recognized by the Department as worthy and helpful in the strengthening of democratic forces throughout the world."

4. Radio Moscow, three years later, during one of its critical broadcasts warning against Moral Re-Armament, made this interesting comment: "Moral Re-Armament is an ideology of the heart and conscience which seeks to supersede the class struggle by the eternal struggle between good and evil."

5. Rear-Admiral Richard E. Byrd, the polar explorer, on the eve of his departure for the Antarctic in 1955 said to the press, "Moral Re-Armament, the fight for a new world, strong, clean, united, should fire the hearts of all red-blooded men and women and stir their wills to action."

6. Robert Schuman, the French statesman, gave this description in his introduction to the French edition of Buchman's speeches: "If we were being presented with some new scheme for the public welfare or another theory to be added to the many already put forward, I should remain sceptical. But what Moral Re-Armament brings us is a philosophy of life applied in action. To begin by creating a moral climate in which true brotherly

14

unity can flourish, overarching all that today tears the world apart — that is the immediate goal."

7. Don Luigi Sturzo, Italian Catholic priest and political philosopher, wrote: "Moral Re-Armament can be compared with the great struggles against slavery and feudalism. It is a call to defense and to conquest, effectively carried out on the moral plane. It is fire from heaven which must kindle into flame the hearts of all men."

8. The Chaplain of the U.S. Senate, Dr. Frederick Brown Harris, wrote: "Moral Re-Armament is a global crusade to win the world to the actual practice in individual lives of the New Testament standards of purity, honesty, unselfishness and love. It is stressing the Gospel truth that tomorrow's hope lies in changed individuals whose ruling passion is not to get but to give; who find life by losing it, and thus discover the only path to fulfillment."

9. The House of Representatives' Committee on Foreign Affairs reported in 1965 through its Sub-Committee on International Organizations that MRA's objectives were: "To bring about a massive transformation of character and motive in men and nations, so that democracy may be strengthened in the free world, the Communist world is won to a moral ideology, and science and technology are used to serve and not destroy the human race."

10. The Negro publication of Washington, D.C., the *Afro-American,* gave this summary from its viewpoint: "Moral Re-Armament is not a political faith, not a religion, but a way of life. You do not join it, you do not resign from it — you just live it. It is the only force in the world today able to end the struggle of class against class, of race against race, and East against West."

11. Peter Howard, the British author and playwright, who at Buchman's death in 1961 spearheaded MRA's development in the next four years, declared: "Moral Re-Armament stands for faith in God; sound family life; industry where people are more important than profits, work as important as wages, service as important as salary; a society which recognizes that class war, with the selfishness of the Right, the bitterness of the Left, is too small and too dangerous for our times; a national goal and aim which all can love and share."

12. Recently J. Blanton Belk, Executive Director of MRA in the United States, summed up essential facts about MRA as follows: "Moral Re-Armament can best be described as an expeditionary force from all faiths and races engaged in a race with time to modernize the character and purpose of man. It is love of home, homeland and humanity. It is absolute moral standards as a compass in personal and national life. It is the firm conviction that enough God-loving men and women can be found who, by example and dedication, will provide leadership whose aim is to right what is wrong in the world. It is not a religion, nor a substitute for religion, nor a sect. It is a non-profit, charitable work financed by people from all walks of life."

Certain basic points emerge from these definitions.

1. One of them was expressed by the American admiral who said, "Moral Re-Armament is doing what you have always known in your heart you ought to be doing — and doing it all day, every day." MRA is not a strange new doctrine. It begins for anyone by living without compromise the best he already knows.

2. "MRA is for everyone, everywhere," said Buchman — "Christian, Jew, Moslem, Buddhist, Marxist, atheist." He added, "Everyone has some moral re-armament. Our job is to up the percentage."

3. A few days before his death, Peter Howard said in a speech, "Moral Re-Armament is not an army, it is a war. It is not a regiment you can join. It is a battle all should fight." You cannot join MRA. By the way you live, think, act, you are part of either the moral re-armament of the world, or of its moral disarmament.

This may be a harsh truth to some in today's world — to those who comfortably hope they are living relevantly merely by belonging to some worthy organization, or to others who imagine that in an age of spectatorism they are not involved in humanity's march to a new age or to disaster.

4. A Canadian publicist said recently, "Moral Re-Armament — what a hell of an inspired name! Just exactly what the world needs, and wants." A glance at any day's newspaper leaves no doubt that the world *needs* a moral force to answer its problems. Beyond that, it is a fact that millions are responding to MRA. It makes sense. It is *wanted* and welcomed. It is an idea whose time has come.

5. Finally, it is only fair to the reader to add that insight into Moral Re-Armament comes best by living that way. As in swimming, theory is grasped faster when you are out beyond your depth. When you are beyond your capabilities, taking on what needs to be put right in the world, Moral Re-Armament is as normal and natural and necessary as breathing.

WHAT HAS IT DONE?

The reaction of most people to a sound and interesting theory is — does it work? Moral Re-Armament has worked to such effect on every continent that in less than thirty years it has become a household word in countries like Germany and Japan, been the subject of concern in Moscow and Peking, built bridges of understanding between hostile nations, races and cultures, and given the impetus to certain great events which have shaped the history of freedom and democracy. Here are some highlights of the record.

1. Moral Re-Armament was introduced in May 1938 by an American, Frank Buchman, at a meeting at East Ham Town Hall, in East London, cradle of the British labor movement.

2. On June 4, 1939, it was launched nationally in the United States at Constitution Hall, Washington, D.C. The occasion was marked by messages from President Roosevelt, former President Hoover, General Pershing, leaders of the Cabinet, industry and labor, and 240 Members of the British House of Commons and other world notables. (See Part Three)

3. At the Hollywood Bowl on July 19, 1939, 30,000 attended the inauguration of Moral Re-Armament on the Pacific Coast. In early December

a series of national broadcasts took place participated in by Admiral Richard E. Byrd, Senator Harry S. Truman and Speaker of the House William B. Bankhead from the United States, and from Britain by the Earl of Athlone and Herbert H. Elvin, Chairman of the British Trades Union Congress.

4. During the early years of World War II MRA became a force supporting the fighting strength of the free nations, especially on the home front. In the fall of 1941 a patriotic revue entitled "You Can Defend America" began a 36,000-mile tour of the United States, sponsored by governors, mayors and civilian defense councils. Two million copies of a handbook with the same title and the theme of "Sound Homes, Teamwork in Industry and a United Nation" were distributed. General Pershing wrote the foreword. The War Department's Bureau of Public Relations described the handbook as "possibly the most challenging statement of this nation's philosophy of National Defense that has yet been written." (See Part Three)

5. The revue and handbook inspired similar productions in Canada, Britain and Australia. The *Army and Navy Journal* of May 6, 1944, wrote: "An important factor in building a fighting spirit on both battlefront and home front has been the program of Moral Re-Armament. In Britain MRA has played a distinctive part in toughening the spirit of the people. Though some of its leaders have undergone imprisonment and death, it remains a bulwark for a liberated Europe. We are fighting a war not alone of arms but of ideas. The victor must be strong in both." (See Part Three)

6. In 1942, through the cooperation of the Governor of Michigan, buildings on historic Mack-

inac Island, at the confluence of the Great Lakes near the Canadian border, were made available for the opening of an ideological training center — first of its kind in the non-Communist world. The center became the scene of conferences to which representatives came from more than 100 countries.

7. With the coming of peace, MRA's directors, reinforced by a score of their personnel specially released from Army service by General Marshall and Secretary of War Stimson "in the national interest," were able to step up their programs aimed at the safeguarding of freedom in the ideological struggle.

8. Central to this post-war world advance was the purchase in early 1946 at Caux-sur-Montreux, Switzerland, of the Caux Palace Hotel and its conversion into the nucleus of a second world ideological conference and training center with special emphasis on Europe, the Middle East and Africa.

9. In the years 1947-50 General Lucius D. Clay and General of the Army Douglas MacArthur, U.S. military commanders in occupied Germany and Japan, cooperated in arranging for delegations from those countries to visit the MRA training centers at both Caux and Mackinac — the first major delegations from former enemy nations to participate in international conferences.

10. A feature of Caux's early years was the stream of industrial delegations which attended from Germany, Italy, France and Britain. Workers by the thousands, employers by the hundreds, Communist Party officials by the score spent days or weeks at the assembly and found there a new dimension of industrial unity and responsible citizenship.

11. For example, from France came Robert Carmichael, President of the Jute industry, together with textile workers. Carmichael found new motives as an employer. He said later, "MRA meant for me to make the passion of my life not money or power, but a remade world." Carmichael met with Maurice Mercier, head of 600,000 textile workers. Mercier, a Marxist and former Communist, was convinced that Carmichael had changed. The resulting agreement between employers and union brought a 16 percent pay increase for the 600,000 workers and a corresponding increase in productivity throughout the industry. Commenting on this new spirit several years later, Mercier told the press, "Not one cry of hatred, not one hour of work lost, not one drop of blood shed. That is the revolution to which Moral Re-Armament challenges workers and management alike."

12. After World War II the coal industry in Britain, key to economic recovery, was the focus of an intensive MRA campaign. A task force with a stage play *The Forgotten Factor* was invited to 150 coal mines. After a few months Harry Lockett, a member of the National Executive of the National Union of Mineworkers, summed up the effects: "When Moral Re-Armament comes in, Communism goes out, production goes up, absenteeism goes down. This spirit in every coal field would ensure national recovery."

13. In 1949 Communist-trained dockworkers engineered the disastrous *Beaverbrae* strike, costing more than 600 million dollars. Two years later MRA-trained dockers, including some who had led the strike, prevented a second stoppage aimed at paralyzing the economy. During the next crucial

years these men gave a new positive leadership on the British waterfronts.

14. In the German Ruhr, Communism's primary continental target, the Kremlin suffered through MRA a reverse which played a major part in averting a Communist takeover. In 1948 three German Communists went to Caux and promptly left the Party. One by one the Communist veterans who were sent to bring them home did the same. The impact of these defections caused a reshuffling of the entire Communist hierarchy of West Germany.

15. In a gesture of panic, the Party issued an order forbidding its members all contact with Moral Re-Armament, thus reversing for the first time since the October Revolution their basic tactic of infiltration. Hubert Stein, a member of the Executive Committee of the German National Union of Mine Workers, stated in June 1951: "In the last three years the number of Communists on the Works Councils of the Ruhr has dropped from 72% to 25%. The main credit must go to MRA."

16. Chancellor Adenauer became convinced of Moral Re-Armament after watching its impact in the Ruhr. With his whole family he attended a conference at Caux. Later he said, "We need an ideological concept superior to Communism. I welcome the fight of Moral Re-Armament, beyond every difference of class, race and nationality for the preservation of peace and freedom." (See Part Three)

17. France's Foreign Minister Robert Schuman also took part in Caux conferences. He found there what he described as "a school where Christian principles are not only applied and proven in the relationships of man to man, but succeed in

Combined touring casts of "Up With People" setting off from Estes Park, Colorado, July, 1966.

The Colwell Brothers of Hollywood Paul, Ralph and Steve who sparked "Sing Out '65", wrote many hit tunes of the show. They sing in 48 foreign languages.

General Eisenhower receives the cast and tells them
"I am proud and thankful for you. If we could wake
up people to what you are singing about we would
have a nation that could stand as an example for all."

15,000 in the Hollywood Bowl give "Sing Out '65" a
rousing send-off on their tour of Japan and Korea.

In the bitter aftermath of the Watts riots 2,500 high school students roar their approval of "Sing Out '65."

The University of North Carolina is one of the many campuses visited by the casts as they cross the country.

At the U.S. Air Force Academy the cadets chee

Midshipmen at the U.S. Naval Academy give a "hats-in-the-air" during an unprecedented 31-minute ovation.

hrough 8 encores. *The cast is invited for a third visit.*

*Men of the 9th Infantry Division at Fort Riley, Kansas,
dip their guidons and climb on shoulders at the finale.*

Anti-American students pack a performance at Waseda University, Tokyo. They cheer, stay to talk. "If this is America," they say, "we are for it. What's our part?"

Prime Minister Sato of Japan congratulates cast after performance in Tokyo's Metropolitan Gymnasium.

*"You have erased a pacifist image of American youth"
was the response of U.S. troops on Korea's 38th Parallel.*

*Korean Prime Minister Chung and family applaud
the cast in Seoul. With them is U.S. Ambassador Brown.*

Maj. Gen. Rowny, Commander U.S. 24th Infantry Division, presents Blanton Belk with Order of the Lion in appreciation for what the cast gave his troops.

Chancellor Ludwig Erhard, host to the "Sing Out" cast in Germany, gives a reception in Bonn to welcome them.

"*Do carry these values of freedom right across Germany and Europe,*" *said Dr. Adenauer to the Americans.*

14,000 in Westfalen Halle, Dortmund, take part in the finale as hundreds of young Germans rush on stage.

Chancellor Klaus, who invited "Sing Out '66" to Austria, is given Western bolo tie at Chancellery reception.

Information Minister Manuel Iribane, host to "Sing Out" in Spain, says, "You have won every heart."

2,000 young Puerto Ricans, who cheered "Up With People," now take part in Sing Outs around the island.

Pablo Casals, the great cellist, receives the cast. He spoke of their music's "inspiration and delicacy."

"Your work could only have been inspired by that power which the Almighty gives mankind," says Sir Clifford Campbell, Gov. Gen. of Jamaica as he receives cast.

General R. W. Porter Jr. (2nd left), Commander U.S. Army's Southern Command, is cast's host in Canal Zone.

Foreign Minister Fernando Eleta of Panama: "We've seen unity of spirit between North and South America."

"Your production is excellent, but the intent and purpose behind it is even more significant," says President Leoni of Venezuela after the premiere in Caracas.

Cardinal Quintero presents cast members with medals of Venezuela's patron saint, saying, "I applaud your idea, the real apostolate of fraternity for the whole world."

The young Americans sing for Mexico's Education Ministry staff and teachers. "A new type of youth to answer hatred, fear, greed and poverty," wrote Novidades, largest Mexican daily.

Japanese, Korean and Chinese youth perform in "Let's Go '66" on Hong Kong streets during Asian tour.

"Harambee Africa," a production of African youth inspired by "Sing Out", sings for Kenya's Pres. Kenyatta.

Emperor Haile Selassie I of Ethiopia is welcomed at the gala premier of "Harambee Africa" in Addis Ababa.

overcoming the prejudices and enmities which separate classes, races and nations." (See Part Three)

18. Schuman, Adenauer and other Frenchmen and Germans who found mutual trust and common objectives through MRA "built a bridge of understanding across the Rhine." The Schuman Plan was a practical demonstration of this trust and became the cornerstone for the remarkable development of economic cooperation in Western Europe. Said Helmuth Burckhardt, Chairman of the Advisory Council of the Coal and Steel Pool of the Plan's High Authority: "The framework and organization we have been able to set up have sprung in large measure from the ideas of Caux."

19. In the summer of 1950, by invitation of Moral Re-Armament and through the coooperation of General MacArthur, Japan's first major postwar delegation to the West visited Europe and the United States. The Japanese leaders, including the Mayors of Hiroshima and Nagasaki, were received by Vice President Barkley and government leaders in Washington. Addressing both Houses of Congress, the Japanese expressed regret "for Japan's big mistake" in "breaking a centuries-old friendship" by the war.

20. The Japanese visit produced a deep impression in America. The Senate gave an unprecedented four standing ovations. *The New York Times* of July 29, 1950, commented, "For a moment one could see out of the present darkness into the years when all men may be brothers." The delegation's call on Ambassador Warren R. Austin, chief U.S. spokesman at the United Nations in New York, was made the occasion for his public proposal that Japan be received speedily into the world body.

21. On their departure from San Francisco for home the Japanese issued a press statement:

"The millions in the Far East must be presented with a philosophy and way of life so appealing that totalitarianism will lose its lure. Russia has advanced in Asia because the Soviet Government understands the art of ideological war. It fights for the minds of men. We appeal to the governments and peoples of the West to do the same — to make themselves experts in the philosophy and practice of Moral Re-Armament, which is the ideology of the future. Then all Asia will listen."

22. At the Japanese Peace Treaty Conference at San Francisco in 1951, the French delegate, Foreign Minister Schuman, told Buchman, "You made the real peace with Japan two years before we signed it."

23. In the United States at the end of 1950 a total collapse of negotiations between the management of National Airlines and the Airlines Pilots Association was threatening the future of the airline and causing concern throughout the industry. MRA provided the means by which the deadlock was broken. The Chairman of the Civil Aeronautics Board made a public statement on May 1, 1951:

"To those familiar with the long history of this bitter and acrimonious dispute, the transformation in the attitude of the parties from one of suspicion and hostility to one of mutual cooperation and trust has been little short of miraculous. In effecting a settlement of this bitter struggle, Moral Re-Armament has performed an invaluable service, not only to the aviation industry, but to the country as a whole, by pointing a way toward a solution of the broader problem of labor-management relations."

24.   During 1952-53 an international MRA force visited India and Ceylon at the invitation of national leaders of those countries. Of this visit Sir Claude Corea, Ceylon's Ambassador to Washington, wrote, "The two great events in Asia since the war are the granting of independence to 500 million people and the coming of Moral Re-Armament to our continent."

25.   In 1955 a "Statesmen's Mission" of 200 made a tour of 14 Asian and Middle Eastern capitals from Tokyo to Cairo. In most of these countries they were government guests. They traveled most of the way in chartered U.S. Air Force planes. Criticism was later made that these planes were provided at the taxpayers' expense. In fact, payment was made in full by MRA. (See facsimile of cancelled check, page 214.)

This mission received considerable positive publicity around the world. One news magazine in the United States, however, gave a totally distorted account of Peter Howard's play, "The Vanishing Island," which accompanied the mission. The play was depicted as pro-Communist and anti-democratic — a strange criticism of a drama which was warmly applauded by government leaders of Free China during the mission's visit to Taiwan. To set the record straight the MRA directors inserted the full and accurate account of the play and the response to it in an advertisement in *Time* magazine. (See Part Three)

A senior member of the Japanese Diet, Niro Hoshijima, sent by his Prime Minister to accompany the Mission from Tokyo to Manila, publicly asked the forgiveness of the Philippine people for Japan's wartime atrocities. His action came at a moment when reparations negotiations between the two countries, deadlocked for ten years, had finally collapsed, and bitterness was intense.

26. The Philippine Foreign Minister who was in the audience was the first to grasp Hoshijima's hand at the end of the evening. Negotiations were reopened next day, and within a year the matter was settled. Japan's Vice Minister of Foreign Affairs, F. Matsumoto, credited the successful outcome to the new atmosphere created by the apology.

27. President Ramon Magsaysay of the Philippines, host to the Statesmen's Mission during its Manila visit, told a senatorial friend shortly before his death: "I used to settle my problems by weighing political issues. Since meeting Moral Re-Armament I settle them on the basis of what is right, no matter whose feelings are hurt — even my own. And I have solved most of my problems."

28. Karachi's government newspaper, the *Pakistan Standard*, in an editorial on June 10, 1955, entitled "Statesmen's Mission," said in part:

"The arrival of this mission in Asia marked the advent of a new relationship between East and West — a relationship which is based on absolute equality born of common purpose. Moral Re-Armament deserves to be looked upon by the Muslims of the world as a forgotten page of Islam itself. We need a leadership which has an insight into the latent yearnings in the hearts of our millions. We need legislators who have the courage to make not popular but right decisions. We need a new type of man and woman capable of surmounting petty considerations in the service of the country. We need a new vision and a new spirit. More than anything else we need Moral Re-Armament."

29. In 1953 the vice president of one of the two rival dockworkers' unions in the port of Rio came to an MRA conference, shortly after leading one of the longest waterfront strikes in Brazil's history. This was the start of a transformation of Brazil's docks. Over a four-year period dockworkers trained in MRA cleaned up corruption among the longshoremen, united the warring unions and established democratic leadership, brought a new spirit between management and unions, ended pilfering and bribery in many areas, drastically cut the turn-around time of ships in their ports and upped the standard of living of the waterfront workers.

30. The Brazilian dockers dramatized this transformation in a feature film, "Men of Brazil," shown around the world, and sent delegations to other Latin American countries, to North America and to Europe to make their experience and conviction available on the world's waterfronts.

31. In 1957 one hundred leaders of Nihon Seinendan, Japan's largest youth organization with more than 4,300,000 members, were invited to Moscow by the Soviet Government. MRA's American directors promptly invited them to the Mackinac Island Assembly in the United States for a course of training in the ideology of freedom. They chose Mackinac instead of Moscow.

On their return to Japan, Seinendan candidates who were associated with MRA were elected to their national executive and won a majority of seats. The Communists had confidently expected to win the elections and control the Seinendan. One of their agents confided, "We were defeated by MRA men who could not be bought by money, sex or personal ambition."

32. From Germany in 1959, Chancellor Adenauer commissioned a company of Ruhr miners trained in MRA to take their new play "Hoffnung" (Hope) to France, Italy, Britain and the United States, continuing on to Japan, India, Cyprus and several countries of Africa.

33. There were unforgettable scenes as the Germans took part in America's Memorial Day exercises at Arlington; laid a wreath at Mt. Valerien, Paris shrine where 4,500 French patriots were shot during the Nazi occupation; and stood in silence before the Cenotaph at Hiroshima. In Washington they were thanked by General Lyman L. Lemnitzer, U.S. Army Chief of Staff, for their contribution to the ceremony. Japan's Prime Minister expressed appreciation for their visit's "massive impact, giving ideological clarity to our people." Said French Socialist leader Guy Mollet, receiving them in the northern coal fields, "We will carry this fight through to victory."

34. During the years 1959–60 Moral Re-Armament had a part in securing of the independence of Cyprus through the senior Greeks, Turks and British who came into contact with it in Europe and America, including British Prime Minister Harold Macmillan, the Greek Cypriot leader Archbishop Makarios and Turkish Cypriot spokesmen Dr. Fazil Kutchuk and Raoul Denktash.

35. The first flag of the new republic to leave the country was sent by Makarios to Dr. Buchman at Caux with a message welcoming a five-nation force to the island that November: "My thanks for your contribution to the solution of the Cyprus question. Moral Re-Armament will continue to build a golden bridge between East and West."

36. Prime Minister Nobusuke Kishi of Japan in

1958 paid a visit to nine countries of East Asia and the Pacific — Korea, Australia, New Zealand, the Philippines, Taiwan, Thailand, Malaysia, Burma and Indonesia. The original purpose was to rebuild his country's shattered international trade, but he decided to follow the advice of an MRA-trained senator in expressing regret for the suffering Japan had caused in the war. Kishi called it the "statesmanship of the humble heart." On his return to Tokyo he wrote: "On this trip I was impressed by the effectiveness of Moral Re-Armament in creating unity between peoples who have been divided. I myself experienced the power of honest apology in healing the hurts of the past."

37. In 1960, on the initiative of Saburo Chiba, Chairman of the Japanese Diet's Security Committee, and Shiinji Sogo, Governor of the National Railways, land was purchased near Mt. Fuji for an Asian Assembly Center for Moral Re-Armament. The center was formally opened on October 22, 1962, by Prime Minister Ikeda in the presence of three former Prime Ministers, and members of the diplomatic corps.

38. In the summer of 1960 Communist-inspired rioting in Japan prevented President Eisenhower from visiting the country. At a key point in the violence the MRA-trained leaders of the Seinendan (see paragraph 31 above) refused to yield to leftist pressure and kept their members off the streets. Labor leaders, socialist Diet members and others associated with MRA also secured support for the government from their followers by maintaining order in key areas of the country. "Had it not been for the men and women trained in MRA," Prime Minister Kishi later declared, "Japan today would be behind the Bamboo curtain."

39.   Spearheading the Tokyo riots were leaders of the Zengakuren, national association of college students. Later that summer 30 of them accepted an invitation to the MRA training center at Caux, Switzerland. They were won to a greater ideology by what they experienced there. They put their convictions into a play entitled "The Tiger" depicting their part in the riots and the answer they had found.

40.   They were invited to bring their play to the United States. After publicly expressing their regrets to Eisenhower's Press Secretary James Hagerty at a performance of "The Tiger" in New York, the young Japanese visited the General at Palm Springs. During an hour's talk Eisenhower expressed his amazement over what had transpired and ended by urging them to visit Latin America.

41.   The President of Brazil was so impressed by their convictions he arranged for the Air Force to fly the Japanese to Recife, capital of the riot-torn Peasant League Northeast. The visitors put on "The Tiger" at the largest theater but eager crowds, including hundreds of Communists, forced adjournment to the football stadium.

42.   Heartened by Recife's response, the government provided Navy and Air Force transport 1,000 miles up the Amazon to the river port of Manaus. "The Tiger" force arrived on the anniversary of Castro's Cuban revolution, July 26, and were told to expect a poor attendance because a large Communist rally was to be held that evening. That night the Castro rally drew 44 people. Across the street in Manaus' huge football stadium "The Tiger" played to a wildly cheering crowd of 90,000.

43.   Next day the President of Peru, hearing the

news, cabled them an invitation to come to Lima and "do in my country what you have done in Brazil." In Lima they gave "The Tiger" for students of San Marcos University, oldest in the hemisphere, and a center of violence and agitation. San Marcos students packed out the hall. Thunderous applause followed the final curtain. Then the Zengakuren faced their audience and challenged them to give everything, with them, to a revolution big and potent enough to change both North and South America — and Europe, Asia and Africa into the bargain.

44. Twenty of the most fiery San Marcos youth, including several who had been in the riots against Vice-President Nixon, decided to join the Japanese in their fight. They wrote their own play "El Condor," a powerful drama of the causes of anti-Americanism in the hemisphere, how Communism exploits the errors of one side and the hates of the other, and how an answer might be found through Americans, North and South, joining forces to build a new society and carry an answering idea to the world.

45. "El Condor" played to enthusiastic audiences across Latin America. Then it toured a year in Italy, drawing thousands of Catholic workers and rank-and-file Party members alike, and playing an influential part in bringing back to the Church many who had been won away by Marxism.

46. In Kenya, East Africa, the national hero Jomo Kenyatta became impressed by men of Moral Re-Armament during his 9-year detention by the British at the time of the Mau-Mau uprising. When he became the first Prime Minister, and later President, of independent Kenya he supported the development of a multi-racial and multi-tribal

47

MRA force to answer national problems such as division, bitterness, laziness and corruption, and the wider problems of the continent.

47. While in prison he had seen MRA's film *Freedom,* the first full length movie made by Africans. Kenyatta requested the film's translation into Swahili and encouraged its nationwide showing to 600,000 Kenyans. His brother James Muigai said, "The new thinking it has brought has played a key part in preparing us for effective self-government where men of all races have an equal part to play."

48. In 1960, when the Congo received its independence, chaos, massacres and a Communist-inspired coup threatened the existence of the new state. An international team of Moral Re-Armament was asked by President Kasavubu and Army Commanding General Mobutu to remain when most white foreigners fled.

49. They were asked to give radio programs twice daily over Radio Leopoldville during this crucial turbulent year in order to train all sections of the populace in MRA. The Colwell Brothers, young Americans from Hollywood, sang in several languages and dialects over the air and their songs exerted a powerful influence.

50. General Mobutu asked another of the MRA force, American surgeon William Close, to serve as Medical Director of the Congolese Army. He was made responsible for ideological training for the army, a key factor in the stability of the country.

51. During 1963 Rajmohan Gandhi, grandson of Mahatma Gandhi, the liberator of India, launched a new "freedom struggle" to rid his country of apathy and corruption and to raise a new dynamic, selfless leadership. Young Gandhi dramatized his

aims for this "revolution of character" in a 3,400-mile "March on Wheels" from Kerala in the south through 39 towns to New Delhi. Carried to the attention of millions by mass meetings, press and radio, thousands of young Indians of every background responded to his call for the moral resurrection of their land and continent.

52. As a result of his campaign has come a powerful national weekly *Himmat* (Courage), which is already one of the most discussed magazines in the East; a musical production "India Arise," similar to the Sing Outs in America; and at Panchgani, near Bombay, an MRA training center which shares with Odawara in Japan the responsibility for training a new leadership for Asia.

53. Following the Brazilian revolution of 1964, the government asked MRA-trained men to tackle the damage done in the ports by the subversion and corruption of the Goulart regime. Within one year the income of the port of Rio doubled, due to renewed business confidence and efficiency as corruption, laziness and subversion were cured. *O Globo,* a leading newspaper, reported in March 1965, "The port of Recife has undergone a basic recuperation in eleven months." The government offered the MRA force facilities to extend their work to all 18 ports of Brazil. Their work has also had a positive impact on similar conditions in the port of Montevideo.

54. In the United States from late December 1963 to early March 1964 Peter Howard, British author and playwright and world leader of MRA, made 46 speeches in 25 cities on a lecture tour in which he related Moral Re-Armament to the vital issues of the day. The tour sparked nationwide interest. Cardinal Cushing of Boston, in his fore-

word to the published addresses, described them as bringing "an extraordinary clarity about America and the world."

55.   As a result of this tour, together with a similar one in the spring of '64 through college campuses by Olympic Gold Medalists John Sayre and Richard Wailes, two thousand selected high school and college youth were trained that summer for leadership at Mackinac Island, Michigan, at a "Conference for Tomorrow's America."

56.   This in turn sparked invitations to Howard from 80 American campuses to speak on Moral Re-Armament. In the fall of 1964, shortly before his death, he spoke at seventeen. During the next months Sayre and Wailes led a panel of youth speakers at colleges and high schools. In the summer of 1965 seven thousand students from the United States and overseas took part in a 12-week conference called "A Demonstration for Modernizing America." It was during these weeks at Mackinac that "Sing Out '65" was created.

57.   In November 1966 in England the Westminster Arts Centre was opened as a significant development of London's Westminster Theater. For the past twenty years this theater had been a powerful voice of Moral Re-Armament in the world of drama. From here the plays of Peter Howard and others had been launched to every continent. The new center is designed as a training ground for talent in all aspects of stage and screen to give a moral ideology to millions.

4

HOW DID IT START?

Moral Re-Armament was born in the heart and mind of an American, Frank Buchman. In the spring of 1938, while he was walking on a wooded lane in the Black Forest, the thought came to him, "Moral and spiritual re-armament — a moral and spiritual renaissance for the world."

When in later years he was congratulated on authoring the idea he always refused to take credit. He said that God was responsible for the idea, just as He was responsible for its amazing growth. Buchman was quite clear that Moral Re-Armament was God's manner of speaking to the modern world and that however imperfect were the human beings who accepted and tried to live and give that idea to the world, the sanity, power and spaciousness of God were breaking in on mankind through it.

Buchman first spoke publicly of Moral Re-Armament on May 29, 1938, in East Ham Town Hall, London, cradle of the British labor movement. The speech was widely reported in the world press. *U.S. NEWS* in Washington reproduced it as a full page editorial. MRA was launched nationally in the United States at mass meetings in Madison Square Gardens, Constitution Hall, Washington, and the

Hollywood Bowl in May, June and July 1939. (See Part Three)

What kind of man was Frank Buchman and what experience lay back of his launching of MRA?

He was a Pennsylvanian, born in Pennsburg on June 4, 1878. During his lifetime he was decorated by eight governments — by France, Germany, Greece, Japan, the Republic of China, the Philippines, Thailand and Iran — for outstanding services which he had rendered through Moral Re-Armament to these nations.

At his death in August, 1961, 22 heads of state and Prime Ministers sent messages, many describing the profound effect he had had upon their countries.

Prime Minister Holyoake of New Zealand said, "He has done as much as any man of our time to unite the peoples of the world by cutting through the prejudices of color, class and creed." Carl Hambro, the Norwegian statesman, called him "the greatest man of our age." In Lima, Peru, 60,000 stood in silence in his memory.

Buchman was an American with a deep love for the countryside in which he was reared and for his country. He also had a love for other lands and for every manner of man, which made him listened to and beloved around the earth. The great German newspaper, *Frankfurter Allgemeine Zeitung* called him "the conscience of the world."

He sometimes spoke of four landmarks in his earlier years:

1. In 1908, his liberation from hatred of men who had selfishly stopped his constructive work in a poverty area of Philadelphia. This experience convinced him of God's power to change a man's motives.

In the years immediately following, through his

work with students, staff and faculty of Penn State College, he not only transformed life on the campus, but worked out experimentally basic principles in the art of remaking men.

2. It was during this time that he became convinced of the necessity for seeking and following the guidance of God. "When man listens God speaks, when man obeys God acts, when men change nations change" became the normal experience of his life and work.

3. In 1912, in Canada he gained with clear insight the conviction that Christianity has a moral backbone, that a valid faith involves the acceptance of absolute moral standards and the courage to pursue them.

4. In 1921, at an international conference in Washington, D.C., he decided that his life's calling must be to raise a force of men and women who would live and work unitedly to answer the worldwide breakdown of morals following the First World War and the rise of militant atheism following the Russian Revolution. Buchman resigned from his comfortable college position and embarked in faith on that task.

Between 1921 and 1938, when MRA was launched, Frank Buchman traveled on every continent, raised a worldwide force of men and women in all walks of life committed — whatever their profession or work, to the task of remaking the world — a "hate-free, fear-free, greed-free world."

In the twenties he captured the imagination of many postwar students in the great universities — Harvard, Princeton, Yale, Oxford, Cambridge. Some of them became the nucleus of a team who gave their full time and energies to the development of his work.

Buchman was concerned to create a network of revolutionary lives to change what was wrong in society. He gave no name to his growing force of colleagues, but in 1929 in South Africa the press first began to call the group of Oxford Rhodes scholars traveling with him "The Oxford Group." This label became for the next ten years the name by which Buchman's work was known worldwide.

Confusion has arisen and criticism has sometimes been leveled at Moral Re-Armament as an outgrowth of two quite different products of Oxford University: first, the "Oxford Movement" of the 19th century — a High Church movement within the Anglican church; and second, the "Oxford Oath," a vote of the Oxford Union (the university debating society) in 1934 that the members would not fight for king and country.

This second confusion seems to lie at the root of the myth that MRA (or the Oxford Group) was or is pacifist. Moral Re-Armament has never been pacifist in war or peace. (See statement by Admiral Standley and extract from the *Army and Navy Journal* in Part Three)

Another myth which is sometimes encountered concerning these early years on university campuses is that the Oxford Group was in some way disreputable and was barred by the authorities from Princeton. The truth is that Buchman's challenge to live the faith you profess stirred a backlash from a group on campus who circulated fantastic rumors. An official university committee investigated the matter and unanimously reported the rumors unfounded. It is also interesting to note that five of the original directors of MRA were Princeton graduates. (See letter of U.S. Senator H. Alexander Smith in Part Three)

During the 1930s Buchman's idea spread rapidly and enlisted hundreds of thousands. Canadian Prime Minister R. B. Bennett in 1934 said, "The work you are doing has made the task of government easier, and your influence has been felt in every village and city of the Dominion."

Also in 1934 Carl Hambro, President of the Norwegian Parliament, invited Buchman to Norway. The Oslo daily *Tidens Tegn* reported, "Two months after the thirty foreigners arrived, the mental outlook of the whole country had definitely changed." One result of this was made clear in April 1945 by Bishop Fjellbu of Trondheim, "I wish to state publicly that the foundations of united resistance by Norwegian churchmen to Nazism were laid by the Oxford Group's work."

Buchman's efforts in the 1930s led in many European countries to a similar awakening to the realities of the aims of both Hitler and Stalin, and during World War II to a toughening of men's moral fiber in defiance of the Nazi tyranny. This is worthy of record since the lie is still circulated that Buchman was pro-Hitler and the Oxford Group soft on Nazism. (See in Part Three Associated Press account of the anti-MRA Gestapo Report)

By the mid-thirties Buchman and the Oxford Group were drawing crowds to mass meetings and assemblies — in Denmark, 25,000 in Copenhagen, and 15,000 in Ollerup; 10,000 in Lausanne, Switzerland; 10,000 at an international assembly at Oxford, 25,000 in Birmingham, England; 100,000 at Utrecht in Holland.

By the spring of 1938, when the Japanese were deep in China, Hitler was threatening Czechoslovakia and Poland and the storm clouds were thickening over Europe, Frank Buchman had laid the foundations of his work in thousands of men and women across the world whose commitment was to God and the remaking of the world.

When Buchman voiced the challenge of Moral Re-Armament that spring, the world was ready and eager for it. Millions in the free world welcomed the idea that military re-armament, at last accepted as essential to check totalitarianism, must also be accompanied by a re-armament of the spirits, hearts, minds and wills of men, if freedom was to survive. Shortly before World War II broke out, the editor of the *Journal de Geneve* sent to editors all over the world a special supplement of his newspaper reporting the news of MRA. In an accompanying letter he wrote, "Whatever happens in Europe, Moral Re-Armament remains the only answer to recurrent crisis and the one foundation for reconciliation and permanent peace."

5

HOW DOES IT OPERATE?

It is clear from a brief survey of what Moral Re-Armament has accomplished that it is more than a haphazard effort. People ask, by what means is MRA advanced? How is it organized? How is it financed? Where are its headquarters? Who tells who what to do?

There is no mystery about these matters except, perhaps, how much is achieved with the man-power and means available.

1. *What means are used to advance Moral Re-Armament?* In general, the answer is by every legitimate means — plays, films, radio, television, meetings, conferences, word of mouth, newspapers, magazines, books — in fact, the whole range of modern communications media.

If this does not seem adequate to explain its explosive spread, it should be added that MRA has been described as a contagion, like measles. People catch it from someone else — if that someone has the germs! In a world sceptical of ideals and suspicious of motives, genuine honesty, all-out enthusiasm, unaffected hope and positive conviction surprise, intrigue and impact the average man and woman. Their normal reaction is, "I didn't know there were people like that in the world today," or, "This makes sense, why didn't I hear about it before?" or, "This is what the world needs."

The basic fact is that Moral Re-Armament spreads so fast because first, men and women associated with MRA *live* what they *believe,* and second, it is an idea whose time has come, and people are hungry for it.

2. *How is Moral Re-Armament organized?* MRA is organized differently in every country, according to the needs, customs and laws of that country. The work in each country is also independent and those who lead it are responsible for their own program in their own country.

The organization is always simple and kept to the minimum necessary. The first requirement is normally a legal one, so that MRA can responsibly own, maintain and use the property, finances and any assets entrusted to it.

In the United States, for example, Moral Re-Armament is incorporated under the title, "Moral Re-Armament, Inc.," as a non-profit corporation of the state of New York. It is subject to the requirements of such corporations, and it obtains the same benefits. It has a regularly constituted board of directors, responsible legally and in fact for the operations of the corporation (see next chapter); its accounts are audited and on public file; it publishes an annual balance sheet and budget.

Frank Buchman, who started MRA, was both a man of faith and a shrewd judge of human motives. He was not primarily interested in founding an organization — he said the world had never been so full of worthy ones already. He was interested in a revolutionary force. Those who are today responsible for the direction of Moral Re-Armament have the same conviction. They have maintained Buchman's determination that those who give their full time to Moral Re-Armament should receive no salary. So today no full-time worker around the globe is paid a salary or wages — more about this later.

Similarly Buchman's clear conviction was that "You are in or out of Moral Re-Armament by the quality of the life you lead." It is just as true today that no one can "join" MRA, except by the commitment of his life. The point is not to "get people into MRA" but to get more moral re-armament into people.

To a world which finds security in pigeon-holing everything and everyone this aspect of Moral Re-Armament is sometimes disturbing. Newspapermen will often press the question — "But how many people are there in MRA?" The honest answer is that the only numbers known are those of the directors (15 in the United States), and those who give their full time to MRA — at the end of 1966 some 4,000 around the world and 1,000 in the United States.

Those who give their full time are invited to do so by the directors of MRA or other responsible men and women after careful consideration, interviews, and in the case of younger men and women, with the full permission of their parents. When volunteers offer their services there is a similar thorough check. In every instance the main concern is that an individual is sincere in his or her motives, as well as capable of undertaking the strenuous life involved.

3. *How is Moral Re-Armament financed?* The short answer to this question is, by the gifts, often sacrificial, of a great many individuals and a smaller number of companies and foundations. (See Part Three). In 1965 in the United States, for example, 942 individuals gave more than $100. Over 5,503

smaller amounts were received. 92% of the contributors were individuals, 4% were corporations, and 4% were foundations.

The Corporation of Moral Re-Armament publishes an annual financial statement after the auditing of its accounts by Peat, Marwick, Mitchell and Co.

Moral Re-Armament is listed in the U.S. Treasury Department's Cumulative List of Organizations, contributions to which are deductible for income tax purposes under Section 170 (C) of the Internal Revenue Code of 1954, Supplement No. 1965–66 (January-December, 1965) published by the Internal Revenue Service on page 31.

Sometimes people seem to make a great mystery out of MRA's finances — implying that it is a wealthy organization, which is certainly not true, or that its assets are not adequately accounted for, also demonstrably not true. Since MRA uses similar accounting methods to those of any reputable non-profit organization such as the Red Cross or March of Dimes, what is the reason for any suggestion of mystery?

Probably one answer is that MRA gets more out of a dollar than many do, so its overhead is exceptionally low. Not only do full-time workers, including directors, give their services, needing only to have their expenses covered, but thousands of others give money, offer their services and use of their homes, provide transportation, or food or other gifts in kind.

Another answer may be that while making sure funds are economically used, those responsible for MRA's programs do not hesitate to commit all available resources in big and strategic actions. Each Sing Out company involves the use of 150 people, and transportation over thousands of miles. Assemblies, films, plays and other means often require expenditure of considerable sums of money, but they are deliberate ventures to dramatize an answer for entire nations and continents.

What the public often does not realize is that to take advantage of an opening or to meet a crucial situation — for example the transportation of Japanese youth leaders to Mackinac instead of Moscow (noted earlier), or the response to the recent urgent invitation of "Up With People" to Central America — may exhaust the financial resources available.

Frank Buchman constantly put his faith and the faith of others to the test when he acted on his conviction that "Where God guides, He provides." On one occasion when the Treasurer of MRA warned him a certain project was costing more than the available resources, Buchman wrote back: "I am grateful for your business caution, but I want you to move with me and the people of America in the dimension of what needs to be done, not what we think we can do. I want you to help me always to live at the place where I rely not on what I have, but on what God gives. It is such freedom, and it works."

It is no different today. The directors of MRA, having given everything themselves in an all-out effort to remake the world in time, live with a sense of urgency and constantly have to respond to needs and opportunities seemingly beyond current resources of money and manpower. That is the road not only of faith, but of growth and maturity. God has honored the stretching of heart and mind with the added means to make the impossible possible.

4. *Where are MRA's headquarters?* There is no

world headquarters. Each nation has its own. In the United States there are several such centers, each with its own function.

The corporate headquarters and finance office is in New York, at 112 East 40th Street, a building given in 1965 by a New York businessman to meet expanding needs. The center for publications is in Los Angeles, at 833 South Flower Street. There are also centers for various purposes in other cities — for example, an embassy-type residence in Washington, D.C.; a home in Santa Fe which has become a focus for a rapidly expanding program among the American Indians; an estate in Mount Kisco, N.Y., serving as the administration center for a rapidly developing "high school on the road" for high school students traveling with Sing Outs; a ranch near Merced, California, which is being developed as a youth training center. At Tucson, Arizona, is the coordinating center for all the programs in America.

Until recently MRA owned a beautiful conference center on Mackinac Island, Michigan, capable of housing 1,000 at a time. The Sing Out explosion has resulted in MRA's outgrowing this facility and it is now owned by Mackinac College, an independent four-year liberal arts college founded to provide a strong academic education together with training in the moral and spiritual qualities which leadership requires in the modern age.

Mention has been made earlier of the MRA conference centers in Caux, Switzerland, and Odawara, Japan. These are designed for international and inter-continental programs. In most great cities of the world there are MRA headquarters, of various size and function — in Ottawa, London, Paris,

Bonn, Copenhagen, Stockholm, Rio, Bombay, Melbourne, Nairobi, and so on.

5. *Who tells who what to do?* In so far as matters of conscience and belief are concerned, MRA stands for the full freedom of every man and woman to decide and to act on his own and according to the teachings of his own church. There is no dictatorship in MRA.

As far as programs of common action are concerned, involving operational strategy and tactics in various countries and continents, those responsible are the directors, members of the councils of management, or whatever the term may be in each country.

In the United States, for example, the directors and any whom they may include or consult, are responsible for planning programs, training, development of manpower, facilities, publications and initiation and oversight of every facet of the work. How do they accomplish this? Much travel, correspondence, countless phone calls, and conferences big and small are involved. Most individual directors have specific responsibilities — for example, finance, publications, the Sing Out program, a geographical area and so on. But beyond that, all are committed wholeheartedly to the fullest responsibility for all that is involved in the creating of a hate-free, fear-free, greed-free world under God.

This commitment is a very practical and definite factor in the lives and work not only of the directors, but of every man and woman, young or old, who gives full-time to the work of Moral Re-Armament. It underlies the truth about MRA which Frank Buchman often expressed — "leadership goes to the morally and spiritually fit." There is always space in the councils of MRA for those who have conviction, inspiration, insight, information. No hierarchy of age or experience exercises a human control to prevent the unexpected, untried or unusual from breaking through. For example, much of the initiative for the Sing Out program comes from the youth themselves.

Where then do control and direction play their part? Moral Re-Armament stands for absolute standards — of honesty, purity, unselfishness and love, and their application in affairs, large and personal, as God gives a man or woman to see what is right. So everyone who is wholeheartedly associated with MRA lives under authority — the authority of God. They take seriously the prayer often on the lips of Christians, "Thy kingdom come, Thy will be done on earth" — not as a pious hope for the future, but as a motive for living today. It certainly does not mean that they are saints. But it does mean that they have a great common commitment and accept a common authority and discipline.

This is the basic reason why Moral Re-Armament operates efficiently with a minimum of organization. There is as much variety and individual character in the men and women of MRA as in mankind itself. There are as many opinions, attitudes, backgrounds, tastes and points of view. But the common acceptance of the aim of shaping the world as God means it to be makes it a great deal simpler to resolve differences, reach decisions and inspire united action. It is rather like the difference between a team of athletes all-out to win, and a team merely playing a game. Or between a nation in a war for survival, and a nation preoccupied with its own affluence.

6

WHO IS IN CHARGE?

Those who are responsible for Moral Re-Armament in the United States are its directors. They numbered fifteen at the close of 1966. Like all those who give their full time to the work of MRA they receive no salary.

They come from all sections of the country and range in age from the late twenties to seventies. Their average age is 45. Their backgrounds and experience are equally varied — business, government, law, medicine, education, journalism and the military.

They have in common a commitment of heart, mind, energies, time and possessions to the remaking of the world. Between them they have had close to a century of experience in developing MRA programs in Europe, Africa, Asia and Latin America, in addition to their leadership of Moral Re-Armament in America.

The fifteen directors are assisted by an Operating Committee of 45 members who represent every facet, both of Moral Re-Armament's program and of national life.

Here are brief profiles of each director:

J. BLANTON BELK, JR. — *Executive Director*
Born in 1925 in Orlando, Florida and raised in

Richmond, Virginia, he attended Davidson College and the University of North Carolina before enlisting in the Navy and serving as a PC boat officer in the Pacific during World War II.

His service with Moral Re-Armament began in 1946. He was on the personal staff of Dr. Frank Buchman with whom he traveled extensively, gaining an intimate knowledge of men and affairs in many parts of the world. A close colleague of Peter Howard until the latter's death, he was at the heart of Moral Re-Armament's advance in Europe, Asia and Latin America.

As Executive Director in the United States, Mr. Belk has been primarily responsible for the explosive growth of Moral Re-Armament during the past three years. He was Chairman of the Demonstration for Modernizing America at Mackinac Island in 1965, where the Sing Out program was born.

He is married to the former Elizabeth Wilkes of Summit, New Jersey. They have one daughter, and make their home in Tucson, Arizona.

DONALD P. BIRDSALL — *Treasurer*

Born in 1916 in Brooklyn, and educated in Westfield, N.J., he was with the Columbia Broadcasting System for five years and secretary to its Executive Vice President. He commenced full-time service with Moral Re-Armament in 1939.

From 1942 to 1945 he served in the United States Army, being attached to headquarters of the first amphibious force launched in the Pacific, and stationed for sixteen months in the Aleutian Islands and later at Headquarters, Alaskan Command.

For many years Mr. Birdsall directed the work of Moral Re-Armament on the West Coast. As Treasurer he has been primarily responsible during the past three years for the rapid expansion of the financial basis of the work in the United States.

He married Susan Manning of Pasadena, and has a son and a daughter.

Paul S. Campell, M.D.

Born in Vegreville, Alberta, in 1912, he graduated from the University of British Columbia with the B.A. degree and from the University of Alberta, M.D. He served his internship and residency at the Henry Ford Hospital in Detroit.

From 1942 he was personal physician to Dr. Frank Buchman and accompanied him to many parts of the world. He has taken a leading role in the training programs of Moral Re-Armament, particularly at the World Assemblies held during the past twenty years at Caux, Switzerland and Mackinac Island, Michigan.

Dr. Campbell has lectured widely on both sides of the Atlantic and is the author of numerous articles, pamphlets and books. These, together with three books, *Re-making Men, America Needs an Ideology* and *Effective Statesmanship,* written in collaboration with Peter Howard, have been translated into fifteen languages.

His wife is the former Annejet Philips of Eindhoven, Holland. They have two daughters.

William T. Close, M.D.

Born in 1924, he received his early education in France, at Harrow School in England, and at St. Paul's School in Concord, New Hampshire, leaving Harvard to serve three years as an Air Force pilot in the European Theater during World War II.

He received his M.D. in 1951 from Columbia College of Physicians and Surgeons and became

Senior Surgical Resident at Roosevelt Hospital, New York.

Since 1960 Dr. Close has traveled widely in Africa, particularly the Congo where he has worked with the government in the development of medical services, and MRA training programs for civilian and military personnel. Through his friendship with many African leaders he has an intimate knowledge of the continent.

He is married to the former Bettine Moore. They have one son and three daughters and have their residence in Greenwich, Connecticut.

GEORGE L. EASTMAN

Born in Potsdam, New York, in 1887, he has long been one of Southern California's business leaders. The George L. Eastman Company, which he started in 1911, became the largest construction materials business west of Chicago. He founded Security Materials Company in 1934.

He was successively the first President of the Hollywood Businessmen's Association, President of the Hollywood Chamber of Commerce, and President of the Los Angeles Chamber of Commerce. In this last capacity in 1928 he was primarily responsible for securing urgently needed Federal legislation to construct Hoover Dam to provide water for the Pacific Southwest. In that year he was honored as "Los Angeles' Most Useful Citizen."

He also served as a director of the California State Chamber of Commerce and was a founder of the Hollywood Bowl, in which capacity he took a leading part in 1939 in the launching of Moral Re-Armament on the Pacific Coast.

Mr. Eastman became closely associated with the development of Japanese-American relations, and in

1965 the Japanese government recognized those services by awarding him the Order of the Rising Sun, its highest decoration for foreigners.

He married Pauline Alber of Hollywood and has a son and daughter and three grandchildren.

BASIL R. ENTWISTLE

Born in London, England in 1911, and a naturalized citizen of the United States since 1950, he is a graduate of Oxford University, B.A. and M.A. and with a Diploma in Education.

From 1935 to 1939 he spent two years in China and Japan and two years in Europe, traveling, reporting for the press, and as an aide to Dr. Frank Buchman.

He served in the United States Army and Air Force in Europe during World War II, and was commissioned in the field and awarded the Bronze Star. He was editor of several Air Force publications.

During 1950-58 Entwistle developed the program of Moral Re-Armament in Japan at the invitation of Japanese political and industrial leaders. In 1965-66 as first Chairman of the Board of Trustees, he prepared the founding of Mackinac College in Michigan.

He is married to Jean Barker of Louisville, Kentucky. They have one son and a daughter.

ROBERT H. HOGAN

Born in New York in 1926, he studied at the College of the City of New York and entered his family's chemical business.

During World War II he served with the 16th Cavalry Group Headquarters in Europe. At the end of the war, concerned for America's future world role, he relinquished his business interests in order to devote himself to bringing about a revolution of national character and purpose throughout the country.

Hogan's special field of responsibility has been the financial and administrative development of Moral Re-Armament in the United States. He has also traveled extensively with task forces in Europe and Latin America.

Married to the former Katherine Ann Wilkes of Summit, New Jersey, he has one son. They reside in Greenwich, Connecticut.

STEWART V. LANCASTER

Born in Louisville, Kentucky in 1927, he enlisted in the Naval Air Force Cadet program during World War II, and was commissioned an Ensign. He graduated from the University of Virginia with a B.S. degree in Commerce and Economics, and did graduate studies at the Woodrow Wilson School of Foreign Affairs.

In 1950 and 1951 he served with the Economic Cooperation Administration in Paris. In 1951 he commenced his service with Moral Re-Armament, first in Europe and in 1952 with Dr. Buchman and a task force in India. He spent several years in Asia followed by two years in Latin America.

In 1965 with Robert J. Fleming he launched the publication of PACE magazine, and in 1966 as Executive Editor added the production of books, records and documentary films to its activities.

He is married to Diana van't Hoogerhuijs of Capetown. They make their home in Los Angeles.

JAMES E. MACLENNAN

Born in 1931 in Detroit, after graduation from

high school he entered full time service with Moral Re-Armament and for the next ten years worked in Europe and Asia, including participation with the task force which traveled through the East in 1952-53.

He was a personal aide to Dr. Frank Buchman from 1955 to 1958, traveling with him through six Asian countries in which Buchman was a state guest.

Since 1964 MacLennan has taken major responsibility for the development of Moral Re-Armament's program for youth in the United States, first with Peter Howard on his University lecture tours, then as director of the Demonstration for Modernizing America and in the leadership of the Sing Out task forces throughout the country. He has traveled with the casts of "Up With People" on four continents.

He is married to Carole Currie of Cleveland.

H. KENASTON TWITCHELL, JR. — *Secretary*

Born in London, England, in 1928, he was educated at Dexter and St. Mark's Schools and Princeton University.

After serving with anti-aircraft artillery in Korea, he was commissioned a second lieutenant of infantry at Fort Benning, Georgia, spent a year as instructor in Psychological Warfare, and was appointed aide to the Commanding General at Camp Kilmer, N.J.

Following his discharge from the Army, Twitchell traveled with Moral Re-Armament's task forces in the United States, Europe and Asia, and for two years participated in its development on the African continent from Cairo to the Cape.

Since 1958 he has served successively in the United States as editor of the MRA Information Service and as a regional director on the Pacific

Coast and in Washington, D.C.

His wife is the former Lydia Bentley of Toronto.

EUGENE VON TEUBER

Born in San Francisco in 1932, he graduated *magna cum laude* from the Georgetown University School of Foreign Service. He speaks fluently French, German, Italian, Spanish and Portuguese.

Since 1955 von Teuber has worked in fifteen countries and has traveled with Moral Re-Armament's task forces in Europe, Asia and Latin America. He assumed special responsibility for its advance in Italy, and more recently in Central and South America.

He is married to Barbara Riffe of Los Angeles.

WILLIAM F. WILKES

Born in 1938 in Summit, New Jersey, he was educated at Bucknell University.

Following the interests of his father who was a senior partner in the investment banking firm of Kidder, Peabody and Company, Mr. Wilkes has specialized in the development of the financial program of Moral Re-Armament in America. He has also worked extensively in Europe and Asia, including a tour with Japan's "Tiger" force in Vietnam.

During the past eight years he has assumed overall responsibility for fund-raising in connection with the rapidly expanding "Up With People" operation at home and abroad. He is Director of the Moral Re-Armament Life Income Fund.

He is married to the former Victoria Bedford of Los Angeles.

WILLIAM VAN DUSEN WISHARD

Born in 1930 in Baltimore, Maryland, he was

educated at Webb School in California.

He served as an officer in the United States Army during the Korean War, was wounded in action while leading an Infantry Platoon in Korea's "Iron Triangle" and was awarded the Bronze Star.

Since 1935 he has served with Moral Re-Armament in thirty countries, including three years in Africa training African youth in the Sudan, Ethiopia and South Africa.

With a task force of Japanese students and their play "The Tiger," he traveled during 1961-1962 through Latin America, Europe and Asia, including visits to Cyprus and Vietnam.

For the past two years he has been a director of the Sing Out Program in the United States, and is now Associate Director of Public Relations for Moral Re-Armament.

He married Anne Twitchell of Princeton, New Jersey. They have one son.

JOHN COTTON WOOD

Born in New York in 1917, he attended St. Mark's School, and on graduation from Harvard in 1939 embarked on full time service with Moral Re-Armament.

A co-author of the war-time handbook "You Can Defend America," Wood served in the United States Army from 1942 to 1945, completing his service with the rank of Captain. After duty with the office of the Chief of Staff, and at Fourth Army Headquarters and the Northwest Service Command, he was appointed an instructor at the Adjutant General's School.

From 1946 to 1953 he was personal aide to Dr. Frank Buchman and traveled with him on all five continents. Since then he has worked primarily in the United States and makes his residence in Washington, D.C.

T. GUY WOOLFORD

Born in 1907 in Atlanta, Georgia, he was educated at Emory University where he received his A.B. and LL.B. He then engaged in the practice of law, and is a member of the Georgia State Bar and of the American Bar Association.

Since World War II he has had a major part in the development of Moral Re-Armament Conference centers and other facilities in the United States and abroad. He has also initiated major MRA task force operations in the Southern States.

His residence is in Atlanta, Georgia.

7

WHAT ARE ITS AIMS?

During the nearly thirty years of Moral Re-Armament's development the world has undergone drastic changes, yet the basic objectives of MRA are as valid today as in 1938. In that year Frank Buchman said in an opening address to the first World Assembly for Moral Re-Armament:

"Our aim ever since the last war has been to give a whole new pattern for statesmanship and a whole new level of responsible thinking. Moral Re-Armament's aim is to remake the world and provide those principles of living that cumulative experience has proved to be practical and demonstrable everywhere. MRA goes to the root of the problem — a change of heart."

During the assembly he added these convictions about Moral Re-Armament's task:

"It builds the strong fabric in the nation's life that holds it firm. It makes the nation conscious of the living God. Then family life insures the nation's health and prepares God-governed children who are fit to be citizens. Then education finds its inspiration as teachers and students, morally sane, are taught by God. Then industry takes hope. Capital and labor work together like the fingers on the hand. Government is made easier. For the more men, under God, govern themselves, the less they need government from outside. Taxation goes down as honesty goes up.

"Moral Re-Armament is building a world organism that takes the needs of nations and answers them with men."

The British Press Association asked Buchman to explain MRA and its aims in a New Year's message, January 1939. He said, "MRA stands for a prejudice-free level of living. It stands for a common denominator of immediate constructive action for everyone, above party, race, class, creed, point of view or personal advantage.

"It is God's property — the new thinking, the new leadership everyone wants. It means God in control personally and nationally. It means the knowledge and exact information that God's guidance brings. It is God's gift to bring an insane world to sanity.

"MRA means honesty, purity, unselfishness and love — absolutely, personally and nationally. MRA means power to change people — our enemies as well as our friends — the other fellow and the other nation.

"MRA is good for everyone, but necessary for us. It will help other nations, but most of all our own and ourselves. It will re-arm people and nations against selfish and divisive points of view.

"The aim of MRA is twofold: first, to restore God to leadership as the directing force in the life of nations; and then to work for the strengthening of morale within a country and so build a healthful national life.

"MRA must go to every heart and home throughout the world.

"MRA is a race with time to remake men and nations. It is the ordinary man's opportunity to remake the world."

Fourteen years later, in 1953 at New Delhi, India, Frank Buchman was asked to give a New Year's message to the people of India. He said: "Men are hungry for bread, for peace, and for the hope of a new world order.

"Before a God-led unity every last problem will be solved. Hands will be filled with work, stomachs with food, and empty hearts with an ideology that really satisfies. That is what Moral Re-Armament is out for. It gives faith to the faithless, but also helps men of faith to live so compellingly that cities and nations change.

"A nation where everyone cares enough and everyone shares enough, so that everyone has enough, will pattern a new social and economic order for this and all future generations.

"A nation at peace within itself will bring peace to the world.

"A nation which makes what is right regnant in personal, industrial, political and national life will pioneer the next historic step of progress and destiny for all mankind."

As Moral Re-Armament was launched in America a pamphlet entitled "The Golden Age" was widely distributed, outlining the kind of world it aimed to create. The author came from a worker's home. (Full text in Part Three). The pamphlet began: "Three great tasks confront this generation: to keep the peace and make it permanent; to make the wealth and work of the world available to all and for the exploitation of none; and with peace and prosperity as our servants and not our masters, to build a new world, create a new culture, bring in the Golden Age."

It goes on: "A world in which we can be trusted

with peace because it will not make us soft; with prosperity because it will not make us proud; with liberty because it will not lead to license; with happiness because it will not make us selfish.

"A world in which the humblest citizen and the mightiest nation shall achieve the greatness which consists in making our greatest contribution to all."

On his deathbed, Frank Buchman in August, 1961 summed up the unchanging central objective of his life's work. He said, "I want to see the world governed by men governed by God. Why not let God run the whole world?"

Following Buchman's death, Peter Howard, a right-hand colleague in his battles for twenty years, brilliant British newspaperman, author and playwright, stepped forward to lead the world advance of MRA. On many occasions he voiced Moral Re-Armament's aims, as he saw them.

During a speaking tour of 17 American universities in the fall of 1964, Howard was confronted with a generation eager for a great purpose for their lives. His talks were followed by an avalanche of questions from the students. On one occasion he was asked, "Could you give a concise summary of what the actual goals of Moral Re-Armament are?" He replied:

"Yes, our goals are very simple. We want a remade world. That's the first point. We want a social, economic, and political revolution which enables all men everywhere to have work to do, food to eat, a decent home to live in and a background from which they get a fair chance in life. We believe that all such progress must root in a revolutionary change in the heart and character of men. And we believe that you and I are the best two men to start it."

Intensely practical, Howard interpreted the purposes of Moral Re-Armament in terms of the issues of the times. To another university audience he said, "We must demonstrate that the alternative of a Red world or a dead world is a false alternative. We must show that our purpose as free men is to rebuild the world with an idea big enough to include everyone everywhere, and powerful enough to change the steely selfishness of the extreme Right which creates the acid hatred of the extreme Left. We need to build a new type of man in a new type of age, where the old social, economic and political injustices are resolved by a change in human nature. This is the only radical and real remedy for our times. Those who think we are going to cure the evils of this century while disregarding the character of man are living in a dolt's dreamland. Unless we deal with human nature thoroughly and drastically on a colossal scale, and start with ourselves, man will follow his historic path to violence and destruction that next time may prove to be final."

In his last public speech before his death, Peter Howard said in Buenos Aires in February 1965, "The modernization of man is an urgent necessity. And we must modernize man at a speed to match the age we live in. We can no longer tolerate a time when man, who has become a scientific, technological and industrial giant, remains a moral and spiritual dwarf. We must create a man free from hate, fear and greed and selfishness. We must create a society where strikes, lock-outs, social injustice and unemployment are regarded as unacceptable. We must build a world where wars are as old-fashioned as the dinosaur. We must establish freedom from end to end of the earth, so that dictatorship of class and color seems to our children as remote as the cave-dweller, with his capturing of his mate with a club and a strong right arm, seems to us."

And finally, here is a recent evaluation of MRA's relevant aims for today's generation of youth, expressed by J. Blanton Belk, U.S. Director of Moral Re-Armament, at the Hemisphere Conference for Moral Re-Armament at Santa Fe, New Mexico, January 1, 1967:

"We have reached a period of opportunity and danger, unprecedented in the world. It will take the best of our lives to answer it. We are at a new turn in history when change is accepted as normal. No one, East or West, North or South, wants the world to stay as it is. Millions want the world to change. You have been demonstrating what kind of change is possible, to which everybody responds.

"The world has seen what Russia and China have done with Communism. The world has yet to see what America could do with Moral Re-Armament, if she put into it her wealth of resources, her creative talents, her economic strength, her military might, her manpower and heartpower.

"Moral Re-Armament is not right wing. It is not left wing. It is not a wishy-washy do-gooder middle-of-the-road program. It mobilizes every element in the nation to play its part in the creation of a new order for mankind. It is not a blueprint for Utopia. It is a battle that deals with life here and now.

"The millions must carry the world forward to the dynamic freedom of nations governed by men who are governed by God. God's control of a nation is not only possible, it is lunacy in an atomic world to think in any other terms."

PART TWO

Questions

Anyone who has read thus far will have many unanswered questions. Here is an attempt to answer fifty of the most frequently asked questions, ranging from personal to global affairs. The answers were given on the spot in reply to questions fired at Peter Howard during a speaking tour of American campuses, public opinion forums, service clubs and in press and TV interviews in 1964.

His replies are fresh, informal, lively, straightforward. They were intended to intrigue and spur his questioners to think in a wider perspective and to live at a livelier pace. He was prepared to satisfy the genuine curiosity of his questioners. He was also concerned to impel them into relevant participation in the central battle of the modern age.

The questions sprang out of the themes of his talks which dealt with the moral re-armament of men, nations and continents and tackled the burning issues of the day — the Vietnam war, the "new morality", Communism in Russia and China, Castro's Cuba, questions of race and civil rights, war and peace, education, economics, business and labor, politics and religion.

Q. **Do you get many people calling you utopian?**

A. We get called many worse things than that. But I will tell you the truth. Nobody is more utopian than people who think they are going to get the world straight without dealing with the fundamental of society, which is man. Unless we deal with that, you will have great idealism, great good will, a certain advance, but with the pace of catastrophe outpacing all the time the pace of change.

For instance, at the United Nations, which is a splendid ideal and certainly has a great part to play, you meet men who hate each other's guts. And then they say they are going to make peace. Is that realistic?

Q. **What would happen if the new motive you talk about became dominant in industry?**

A. I think it would lead to a tremendous increase in productivity all over the earth, because men would want to serve and give. I think there would be a fair day's work given for a fair day's wage, and a fair day's wage for a fair day's work. But above all I think there would be a great incentive of service coming out of the hearts of men, so that no worker, no employer would ever rest until every hungry belly on earth was fed.

Q. **What kind of world are you trying to produce?**

A. A world living in full liberty and fulfillment because it is governed by men governed by God, ruling people who look to God.

Q. **How have free men let themselves be used to establish Castros around the world?**

A. Here is a personal illustration. My colleagues and I went to some of the biggest New York investors in Cuba one year before Castro took command. I dared to tell them that Castro was a committed Communist. He was going to take over the country and run America out of Cuba. They said: "You don't understand anything about Castro. We know the reforms he stands for are the right reforms and we're going to stick with him."

Then they asked: "If you wanted to give an ideological answer to Castro on Cuba, how much would it cost?" I answered: "To give the right idea and the moral basis to secure freedom on Cuba would cost a million dollars." They showed me politely out. They gave Castro eight million dollars. Your government gave him fourteen million, and he skinned the whole blooming lot.

Q. How does Moral Re-Armament work in the home?

A. Take my wife and myself. We have three children. We always wanted our children to do what they were told, but we always did as we pleased. Not very convincing. Then, my wife and I often came at things from different angles. She's a woman. I'm a man. She's a Latin. I'm Anglo-Saxon. And whenever we disagreed in the past, I would always say to myself, "Sooner or later she will see reason." Very British. Now I have learned through experience that she sees many things I do not see. I see some things she does not see. In reaching any decision we need each other to find the fullest of truth. So we have learned to work together. We learned to be honest with our children. Where our will crosses God's will, we try to choose God's will. And we find if that's real in our lives, the children are willing to accept it too.

Q. What is honesty for you may not be honesty for me. How can you make this thinking so absolute?

A. I won't attempt to contradict you. All I can say is, if I tell a lie, it is a lie. If you tell one, it may not be. But if I do, it is.

Q. What are MRA's relations with the established churches?

A. It challenges them all with their own truth. Moral Re-Armament is something lived. We aim to see that everybody lives it. As a Catholic friend of mine says: "The Church does not need Moral Re-Armament, but Catholics do." That is our attitude to people in the churches. Some of them like it and some of them hate it. We simply take the view that people in the church should live what they talk about, and we try and hold them to it.

Q. Is there anything the United States could have done considering how powerful, how wealthy we are, that would have made us loved by everybody?

A. It is of course true that some countries are jealous of America. It's no good pretending in my country, if we see ourselves encouraged rapidly out of Asia, out of Africa, out of the places where we once held sway, that we're not somewhat pleased if we see Americans making mistakes. It's not very pleasant, but it's very human.

But I don't think the point is whether America is loved or not loved. I believe that if the whole world rose up today and said, "Good old America," it wouldn't alter the price of cheese. I don't think America knows what the world expects, and rightly expects, of her. The whole world is waiting for America to show humanity how to take the next step forward in human evolution.

Q. Is United States foreign policy tough enough on Communism today?

A. I think the logical outcome of getting tougher and tougher is atomic war. What I want to see is democracy with an ideology that can secure a basis for freedom in the free world. At the moment in many sections of the free world we risk losing our liberty through our own corrupt society. I am not talking about America at this point. I am talking about an ideology that will unite the free world instead of allowing us to tolerate division in our own ranks, and that is powerful enough to capture and win the Communist world. I don't regard that as being tough. I regard it as being sensible. At the moment we lack that arm, so we are forced to the choice of either being tough and risking war, or being soft and risking slavery.

Q. Should Communist China be allowed in the United Nations?

A. There are certain rules of entry. So far Red China has not said she is willing to obey those rules.

I was in Geneva when Vietnam was divided ten years ago. I had to go to the hotel where the delegates were staying. There was a party going on and most of the Western delegates were relaxing. I could not find the man I was looking for, so I went into the back of the hotel and there in a side room were the Chinese. They were dressed in their uniforms. They weren't smoking. They weren't drinking. They were working. I found my friend, and we went to a play of mine that was running there at that time.

I brought my friend back after the theater. The hotel was deserted. There was debris from the party in the front of the hotel. And at the back, there were those Chinese, still at work. Still no smoke. Still no liquor. Next day at the conference, which settled the fate of millions in Southeast Asia, the Chinese ran sixteen circles around the free delegates who had been behaving the other way the night before. They had an ideology, and a plan. They were ready.

If we free men were willing to discipline ourselves voluntarily, and plan intelligently for the world — if we had a superior ideology — I would be ready to have any Chinese met by anybody. But if you ask me at this moment whether I would strongly support the entry of Red China into the United Nations, my answer is, "No, I wouldn't." Not until they agree to obey the rules. If they say they will obey the rules, that is different.

Q. Communism offers the Chinese something to eat. How does Moral Re-Armament go about this?

A. I'll tell you two things of interest. First, that the hungry people there are not the most indifferent to a moral challenge. They know their need of it. It is very often the rich people who are the most selfish. I'm not saying why. I'm reporting observations. Second, we found in the starvation areas along the Kerala coast of India, that when Moral Re-Armament began to work, when villages began to mend their differences and share their water, when people began to work together, there was an instant rise in the productivity of food which was what those hungry people needed. I believe if you get people to live straight, there is enough in the world for everybody's need right now, but not for everybody's greed, and if everybody cares enough and everybody shares enough, everyone will have enough. That is a far more fundamental weapon than using food as an instrument of policy, which is now done on both sides of the Iron Curtain.

Q. **What kind of relationship do you foresee in the future between Russia and China?**

A. Personally I never rejoiced in a great split between Russia and China. That is not because I am a Communist. I am not. But I think in the modern world people who rejoice at colossal differences and splits between powers who both possess atomic might are very foolish. I think that Khrushchev was a pragmatist and a realist. I think he had begun to see certain elements in free society which he wanted for the Soviets. I also think that he was surrounded by people who did not tell him the truth. That is my information. What I would like to see as the intelligent action of free men is the creation of the right revolution so we could say to the Communist world, "Look here. You call yourselves revolutionaries. We in our society have done far more than you to establish equality, to establish justice, to establish prosperity, to establish peace. We have the secret in our own homes, in our own industries, our own communities. Come and participate. It will mean change for you and change for us, but do it."

Q. **What part does education play in building character?**

A. I am fully in favor of better education for everybody. I think ignorance is a great bar to the fulfillment of human character. I think everybody should have a decent home and enough of life's things at least to live decently. But neither environment nor education by themselves create the fullness of character. What I say is that you have got to deal with environment. You need the best in education. But you have also got to deal with the motives of a man's heart and life.

Q. Do absolute moral standards contradict human freedom?

A. I believe passionately in freedom. I'm satisfied, however, that we've got to help people make the right choices. I'm not going to tell anybody what to do. I'm not a dictator. But I'm not going to stand by when I see other people cram their godlessness and relative standards down the throat of the public, thereby rendering the public incapable of making the right choices.

William Penn said years ago — and I regard this as an eternal political truth for all countries, "Men must choose to be governed by God or they condemn themselves to be ruled by tyrants." By that Penn meant that whether men live in liberty or slavery depends on how they make their choices, how they live their lives. And if you get a nation devoted to the proposition of selfishness and number one first, sooner or later the strong man steps in from left or right and says, "For your own good I'm going to control you. And you think what I think and you do what I do." And that's the end of freedom.

I believe that men should be absolutely free to decide. But I think that they need absolute moral standards to decide by. That is why, in my view, absolute morality is the only answer to absolute totalitarianism. That's why I'm for it. I think it's God's will for men to stay free.

Q. Sometimes even now you hear that Dr. Buchman was soft on Nazism. Is it true?

A. It is a lie. One sentence quoted out of context which he allegedly uttered nearly 30 years ago is used against us all: "I thank God for a man like Adolf Hitler who has raised a front-line of defense against the anti-Christ of Communism." I was not there in 1936. I have no idea whether Dr. Buchman spoke as reported. He never met Hitler. And certainly I find it strange that on a day when he was interviewed by 50 reporters, only one so reported him.

I worked closely with Buchman for 15 years. His whole life was dedicated to answering the materialism out of which rose the satanic regime that all decent men hated, and its hideous treatment of the Jews.

I have in my safe the Gestapo instructions declaring that Moral Re-Armament "frontally opposed the Swastika with the Cross of Christ," that it was National Socialism's "avowed antagonist," and was "lending the Christian garment to world democratic aims." (See Part Three)

Now let me read you what other people said about Hitler 30 years ago: "Hitler may go down in history as the man who restored honor to the great Germanic nation and led it back, serene and strong, to the European family circle." That was Winston Churchill in 1935.

Here is Lloyd George: "Hitler is the George Washington of his country."

Does anybody dare suggest that Churchill or Lloyd George were soft on Nazism?

In 1934 the association of national German Jews issued this appeal supporting Hitler: "We welcomed the national rising in January, 1933, because we regarded it as the only way to repair the damage caused in 14 years of misfortune by un-German elements." I hope nobody suggests that the Jewish people, whose blood and bravery still challenge the world's conscience, were Hitler lovers. Of course not. They were simply trying to avoid the gas chambers. Who can blame them?

But remember Buchman, too, had people in Germany. How could he, when needled by this distorted statement, come out and say, as of course he believed: "Hitler is a madman. All the trappings of Nazidom must be thrown onto the rubbish heap of history." Had he said it, everybody in Germany known to have known him would instantly have been destroyed. And indeed many were destroyed.

Q. Could moral absolutism lead to political absolutism?

A. Moral absolutism, its traditional standards of honesty, purity, unselfishness and love that spring from our Judeo-Christian heritage, are the only answer to political absolutism and the absolute finality of atomic war. We need a revolution of the human heart based on absolute moral standards, embracing everyone everywhere and proclaimed and lived in the White House and every home in the United States. I firmly believe Moral Re-Armament is the revolutionary issue of our times. It is the next step for America and the world. If you believe in

God, call it God's weapon for the day and God's philosophy for the century. If not, call it plain common sense. It is neither Left nor Right. It believes in sound homes, teamwork in industry, unity in the nation, a rebuilt world.

Q. Maybe there is no such thing as right and wrong — who is to decide?

A. All right. But if you say that to yourself, you have nothing whatever to say to a Hitler or a Stalin. Hitler and Stalin chose that course. They decided that what suited them was right. If I decide what is right for me and to hell with everybody else, how can I point a finger at any dictator? How can I point a finger at Stalin, who says, "Two million people can be killed because the State needs it," when I say, "If a child's unwanted, let's kill it. Let's have an abortion"? How can I say a word to Hitler, who decides to lacerate, mutilate and torture people who happen to be born Jewish, if in my own life I say, "I'm going to do what I think suits me best, and that is my idea of right and wrong"? Hitler would reply: "That is precisely what I say."

Q. How can you live absolute moral standards unless you are perfect?

A. I do not speak of men becoming saints. I am not one. I wish I were. I talk of standards to establish correction and direction for an individual or a society. The North Star is in the sky. No ship has reached it. For centuries mariners have surveyed it and set a fresh course. We need absolute standards to know where we have gone wrong and where we are heading.

Q. Can you sum up MRA as the absolute standards?

A. I know a distinguished surgeon. He was taught

each morning for three years to wash his hands before surgery. Washing was necessary. But it was not surgery. In the revolution of Moral Re-Armament we are engaged in a task of world surgery for which all need clean hands. In the same way, an architect or builder needs absolute standards of measurement to build a house. Without them the building collapses. It takes more than measurements to put up the building. It takes men, money, bricks, cement and steel. Yet, without absolute standards all that man builds is chaos, in a house or in society.

Q. Would you care to discuss your concept of sexual morality and its rational basis?

A. When I got married, I was married in a church, and I made certain promises to my wife that I'd be loyal and true to her alone, for better, for worse, for richer, for poorer, in sickness and in health, till death us do part. That's a very solemn undertaking, and I think it means precisely what it says, neither more nor less. Nobody has to take such an oath before God, but if they do, I think that is exactly what they should live.

Second point. I have two sons and a daughter. I've just been in Canada where a well-known man up there says he hopes his daughter has sexual experience before marriage and he prefers a bed to a sofa. I don't feel that way. I think men and girls should enter into marriage straight and pure. I don't think playing with yourself is pure; I think it's dirty. I don't think people with perverted habits are more or less wrong than people with unperverted habits, but they can be cured. I don't believe in rationalized impurity. I believe in God-guided purity.

Q. What is your view on intimate relationships?

A. I don't believe in free love, if that is what you are talking about, because I have seen too much misery caused by it. I don't believe that the exploitation of another person's body because it is a different sex, is any more noble than the exploitation of another person's labor because he is a different color. Very simply, I believe in purity. I don't think that God, who gave a man and woman instincts, is so impotent that He cannot teach them to control them. If you suggest that I don't know what I am talking about, I am a father and grandfather. Put that in your cigarette case and rattle it.

Q. There are many religious sects, each of them interpreting the word of God in their own way. Would you clarify a general content that all religions might adhere to?

A. I would say that absolute honesty is common to every denomination, wouldn't you? Is everybody who goes to church absolutely honest? Absolute honesty, absolute purity — that's a difficult one. It's interesting that when you talk to people in Britain, if you get to absolute purity, some of them start laughing. A good friend of mine called Streeter, who was one of the great Oxford professors, talking to an audience rather bigger than this, said, "Laughter is the shout of delight with which a fool recognizes himself." But absolute purity, and I mean absolute purity. I tell you frankly if you start talking about purity, people say that you are making an overemphasis of it. I don't. But I don't want to make

93

an under-emphasis of it either. I think calculated, rationalized impurity has done more than any other single factor to destroy family life in my country, and to destroy our heritage.

Absolute unselfishness, where you honestly sacrifice your selfishness for your nation, instead of sacrificing the nation for your selfishness. And absolute love. I don't mean absolute love in a sentimental, lovey-dovey way. I mean loving a man, or loving a nation, or loving a community as they are, but laying down your life to help them become what they are meant to be.

I think that's a good fundamental start for all churches and all faiths. It's elementary, but let's start with the elements.

Q. Do you think it is possible for an individual to be pure, honest and loving, and be an agnostic at the same time?

A. I think a great many agnostics and atheists are more pure, honest, unselfish and loving than certain people who are not atheistic and agnostic. I've met many of them who have said, "I don't believe in God, but I will accept an experiment in absolute moral standards because that's the way I want other people to live." I'm bound to warn you, it's a dangerous experiment, because you soon get to a place where you need some power other than your own mind. But this experimental method, I know from experience, is often the ladder to faith.

Q. What is the difference between Moral Re-Armament and basic religion?

A. There is a symbol called the dollar in this country. Occasionally I see one. It has printed very boldly on it, "In God We Trust." That does not make it a religious emblem. We are not a religion. Most people feel you can join a religion. You cannot join Moral Re-Armament. There is a certain level of Moral Re-Armament in every man, woman and child on earth. Our job is to up the level.

Q. Is Christianity the basis for your ethic?

A. Christ believed in absolute honesty, purity, unselfishness and love. Do the Christians live them? That is the place you have to start if you happen to be a Christian. Otherwise, if you say to a Muslim or a Hindu or Buddhist, "I am a Christian, live like me," they may say, "That is precisely what I'm doing—living like you. I compromise on all my convictions." But if you say to them, "Do you believe in absolute honesty?" they will all say: "Yes." "Then do you live it?" Challenge them to the experimental method. The Almighty will put into their hearts the place where they need to begin. But if you challenge them to that experiment it is as well to have honestly made it first yourself.

Q. If your message is at heart the basic Christian message, why do any churchmen oppose you?

A. Have you ever tried to tackle a pious, ineffective Christian on the subject of changing and living what he talks about? We have had Christianity preached in Britain for a thousand years, from pulpit after pulpit. In terms of the Christian ethic, we have a greater economic advance today than ever before. I thank God for it, and I hope it goes further. But in terms of men's relations with men, communities with communities, older generation with younger generation, we have never been less like the Christian ethic, and we're getting further from it. Something is wrong.

Q. Is the inner voice absolute, or can it be trained or mistrained? What about the Nazi, for example, who obeyed his inner voice and turned in a Jew?

A. The inner voice is very accurate, very down-to-earth and talks your language. It is trained by obedience. But of course you can mistrain it, if you want to. That is why so many church leaders who disbelieve in absolute moral standards, compromise and fail to give the moral direction which is the true job of the Church. They say in effect: "Everybody compromise like us and you'll be more comfortable people to live with."

I don't think that a Nazi who bullied or betrayed a Jew was actually obeying his inner voice. I think he was obeying an ambition to please the boss, and it was the wrong boss. But you don't have to censor the inner voice.

Q. You seek to change the individual. If you change the environment, won't individuals change?

A. Mr. Khrushchev said publicly in Moscow, I think in July or August last year, that after years of socialist experiment he has failed to create the new type of man he needs for Communism. I'm passionately keen to change environment, education and institutions, but by themselves they will not change the nature of man.

Q. Where do you begin with this change in human nature?

A. We were talking the other day to some of the most intelligent men in America. One of them said: "Is it intellectual change you are talking about?" And I replied: "Well, if you worship your intellect before God, that's probably where you need to start changing. If you worship dollars or profit or color or class or race or pet hates before you worship God, that's probably where you need to start changing. Everybody knows in his heart where he needs to start. There is no single pattern."

Q. How do you propose creating this new type of man?

A. I'll tell you how you and I can start doing it. Take a piece of paper right now. First, write down four words—"honesty, unselfishness, love, purity." Then put, in very big letters, "ABSOLUTE." Next, if you believe in God, write: "Listen to Him." He'll tell you what to do — how those absolutes apply to you.

If you don't believe in God, be clear how you want everyone around you to live. Be clear in detail. Then start living that way yourself.

Try this experiment. If you try it and it doesn't work, let me know. But if you have honestly tried, you'll be the first person I have met who could say it didn't work.

Finally, be crystal clear what you and I are living for. In the present tumult, where men are technological and industrial giants but moral pigmies, unless we live for the remaking of the world we have an inadequate aim. Because nothing else will save humanity from destruction. It's difficult, but no aim short of that is valid.

Q. How do you reconcile absolute love with your attitude toward the Communists?

A. We need a revolution big enough to include the whole earth, and powerful enough to change the whole earth. When I first began to apply Moral Re-Armament, I told my wife two or three things she didn't know about me. I've always remembered what she said: "Peter, I think I'm meant to love you as you are but to fight to help you become the man you are meant to be."

That is my attitude to Communist and non-Communist alike. I think Communism, which flatly says it cannot triumph until the myth of God is removed from the mind of man, is a narrow idea. I love the Communists enough to try and include them in something far more spacious and far more revolutionary than a narrow class concept.

I am not against Communists. The biggest anti-Communist in history was Hitler. But he only succeeded in spreading Communism over half the earth. I think free men could create a revolution bigger than these class-war men. But do we care enough to do it? We criticize them, but offer no revolutionary alternative. I think that is lack of love.

Q. Are you a pacifist?

A. No, I am not a pacifist for a very simple reason. I believe there are things in life worse than death. I would personally be quite willing to fight and die to make available to other people the freedom of choice on which the development of the human spirit rests. I think in the present world situation it would be very foolish to strip yourself militarily and expect freedom to remain on earth.

Q. You say we need a massive change of character. Will this happen?

A. I believe it will. We live in an age of the greatest opportunity and greatest danger that ever confronted man. I have faith in the common man in every country. I believe that when he sees that the old, small, deadly hates and fears and greeds that for so long have imprisoned him may actually destroy civilization, he will change. And I believe that change is not only possible, but necessary and even adventurous.

Q. **How long do you think it would be before a new world could happen?**

A. How long? It's a good question. I think it depends on us. I think it could happen very much more quickly than we believe, because everywhere now people are hungry for an answer. And many know that the causes, however good, to which they have given their allegiance, will not in the end prove to be the full cure. I think it could happen quickly. The truth is, that in the last two or three years the resonance and response to our work has been overwhelming. It is growing very fast.

Q. **What do you think about the Peace Corps?**

A. I think the Peace Corps is a splendid idea, and it represents the best idealism in the United States. I salute it. But, and it is a big but, I am not sure that the men and women in it are given adequate training when they are sent forth.

I've met many people in the Peace Corps. They are fine people. I've met many in Asia and Africa who've met the Peace Corps. On the whole they are liked by the Africans and Asians — but they don't change men. What they do is to make friends for America. I'm all for making friends for America, but that by itself is not actually going to meet the challenge of history.

What these underprivileged countries need are revolutionary Americans who go in there and say: "We understand Marx and Communism. We understand you. We've got a far bigger plan for you and your country, and we've got the discipline to see you achieve it." If you can send out a Peace Corps like that, you can win the world.

Q. Do you believe men should give up power and money for the common good?

A. I would far rather see people who are entrusted with power and money use it as God guides. If you cannot be trusted with it, give it up. I did have in my country a considerable influence with my pen. I had a very highly paid job. I gave up both because I thought it was the right thing to do. I am not saying that because I regard it as anything but common sense. It is possible for people to be given a motive greater than personal selfishness or lust for power. It can happen. I believe that people with money should spend it to save civilization, not to amass more wealth, I think we have got to give men a new motive.

Q. Would you care to summarize some of your feelings and opinions on what our government should do in the South American countries?

A. Well, it puts me in the position of being impertinent, but I will answer your question. I think that your government and my government ought to back massively a program of Moral Re-Armament in every country which remains free.

The press of Brazil announced yesterday that I and some friends have just been asked to the Latin American countries. They said they felt it was the answer to the economic and social differences in Brazil. Supposing Washington or

London said to the world, "We are going to stand for the moral re-armament of humanity. Every diplomat we send forth is going to live MRA. Every Peace Corps person is going to be trained to change himself and change the other fellow, and to proclaim an answer to a nation. Democracy, we know, is only as strong as the people who speak in her name. We're going to send forth people who are incorruptible and strong." I think we'd win the world.

I had dinner in Washington two weeks ago with the Brazilian Ambassador, and he had seven other ambassadors from the Latin American countries to meet me—men of varied political views. They all said this: "A whole culture is being torn up by the roots. We have no hope of preserving our European culture that is dear to us unless you come. Will you come?" And I thought to myself, "Here in Washington, why do these people have to say this to a poor benighted visiting Englishman?" It's crazy. Of course it ought to be the normal of the State Department — and of our own Foreign Office. But I'm sure that everybody in both places wants Moral Re-Armament, and I'm sure they don't all live it.

Q. Does Moral Re-Armament have an economic program?

A. Yes, our economic program is very simple: it is madness to live in a world quite capable of filling every stomach with food, of giving everybody a decent place to live, of giving everybody the education and background they must have — unless we tackle these needs swiftly, radically, immediately.

Q. Would you say that your idea of North and

South Vietnam being given a common idea is related to coexistence?

A. I don't think that a field of cabbages can coexist very long with 300 rabbits. I think it does take an idea to beat an idea. I don't think you can answer an idea by bayoneting it or bombing it or even nailing it to a Cross. I think the weakness of democracy is this: we fight economically, we fight politically, we fight militarily if we have to. But the Communists fight politically, economically, militarily, and also with an ideology that reaches out and captures the allegiance of people. Where is the ideology of freedom? Why in the world should the North Vietnamese not be captured by our concept for the world? Because we don't give it to them. The reason we don't give it to them is because we don't have it.

It involves what we live for here, you see. If we are simply living for a decent, prosperous, comfortable, happy life, we haven't got a hope against the Communists. But if free men had an ideology, a concept for the world, and matched it with a discipline that would out-discipline any slave, right, left or center, of course freedom would win the world. And it's the way I believe men are meant to live.

Q. What is your attitude towards nuclear weapons?

A. The proliferation of the atomic bomb is something every sane person must regard with anxiety and realism. If things go on as they are, by 1970 we shall have America, Russia, France, China, Egypt, possibly Israel, Japan and India all possessed of the thermo-nuclear weapon. Sukarno says that Indonesia is going to build one, too. How true that is I cannot say. I know it is true that the United States provided him with a reactor from which thermo-nuclear power can be built. In any event, this proliferation means every honest man must admit that thermo-nuclear war becomes more, not less, likely.

It follows that some power, some nation, some group of nations, must have the intelligence to proclaim a world aim radical and revolutionary enough to include everybody, to change everybody, and to outmode the injustices against which any power might risk a thermo-nuclear assault. I respect the sincerity of some of those who advocate neutralism or unilateral disarmament. But I profoundly disagree with the idea that these attitudes will accomplish anything except disaster.

America, the leader of the free world, needs an idea in her head and an answer in her heart, as well as bombs in both hands. It is up to us to provide the idea and to live the answer. It will mean change, but there is nobody more reactionary and out-of-date than the person who hopes the situation in the world will become different, but remains unwilling to become different himself.

Q. **Does Moral Re-Armament proceed from the personal to the political?**

A. The whole world needs an aim greater than anything Communism or anti-Communism produces. Nationalism is too small an aim. If you want the world to get straight, you cannot be effective in that revolution unless you are at least willing to get straight yourself. But you do not have to wait till you are straight before you can participate in a revolution.

Politics, yes, if you mean by politics the way in which legislation, government, cabinet affect the lives of people. But we would never be a political party, nor would we ever be exclusively for one party. We believe that every party needs this spirit—every single one.

Q. How can absolute moral standards be applied in politics, which is in part the art of compromise?

A. A man in politics must achieve the very best he can with the society in which he is working, and therefore he often has to compound with something less than the maximum. But if every man in parliament refused to compromise with standards of absolute honesty, purity, unselfishness and love, in any situation, we would get far better laws.

Q. What do you think is the fundamental issue in the world today?

A. I do not think the real issue in the world today is between progressives and conservatives. I do not think it is between free enterprise and capitalism, between East and West, between black and white, or even between capitalism and Communism. I think it is between those who believe that God made man and can change him, and those who believe man made God and can abolish Him. I may say that the present confusion is, to my mind, largely the fault of churchmen and professors who often for their own comfort want to cut the standards of the country down to the size and shape of the defeat in which they live.

The issue is between those who would strive to lift humanity up to Christ's size or God's stature, and those who would try to cut God and

Christ down to man's size. The latter would scrap all institutions and practices that are unexplainable to the modern mind. Unhappily, these appear to include chastity, sacrifice and change. I know what I am speaking about for I am one of a generation at Oxford University which first used its brain to kill its own conscience and then used its place and position in society to kill the conscience of a nation.

Q. What is your attitude toward the New Morality?

A. In my day, the apostle of new morality was Aldous Huxley. Later in life he got honest about what had made him tick. I quote from *Ends and Means:* "I had motives for not wanting the world to have a meaning, consequently assumed that it had none, and was able without any difficulty to find satisfying reasons for this assumption. . . . For myself, as no doubt for most of my contemporaries, the philosophy of meaninglessness was essentially an instrument of liberation. The liberation we desired was simultaneously liberation from a certain political and economic system and liberation from a certain system of morality. We objected to the morality because it interfered with our sexual freedom."

Of course, some people say it is of no consequence and that the way we live does not affect the way the nation goes. A book by Dr. J. D. Unwin, called "Sex and Culture," and described by Huxley as one of the highest importance, takes a different view. Unwin is discussing the trends of society and the tides of civilization through centuries of time. Of culture and continence, he says as follows: "Sometimes a man has been heard to declare that he wishes both to enjoy the advantages of high culture and to abolish continence. Any human society is free to choose, either to display great energy or to enjoy sexual freedom; the evidence is that it cannot do both for more than one generation."

Q. **Please relate to us, sir, the actual physical construction of your program.**

A. Sometimes that puzzles me too! We have indigenous movements for Moral Re-Armament inside most free nations and beginning to grow inside nations that are not free. We have 3,000 people who give their lives as full-time workers. We don't take any salary; we share what we have. We finance our work as Washington financed his revolution—on our knees. The accounts are audited in each country and filed for public inspection.

The main force of the work is now literally millions of people in different parts of the world who stay precisely where they are—on campus, in business, in a church, in industry, in politics, on a farm—and carry the philosophy out to the situation they're in and try to make it regnant in their country. We have training sessions all over the world. We have this New Year three assemblies going on in Africa, one in Japan, two in India, two in Latin America, three in the United States, one in Canada, as well as assemblies and plays running in Britain, Germany, France, Italy and the Scandinavian countries.

I think the best description of the work is the one given by Moscow Radio last time they attacked us: "Moral Re-Armament is a global ideology with bridgeheads on every continent and now in its final phase of total expansion throughout the world." But you can't join. If we start a joining organization, we'll become a sect, a club, a party or a church. And that we will never be. We're an idea on the march.

Q. I am told you are anti-Jewish. Is this true?

A. In Italy now there is a play of mine running. It is called "Through the Garden Wall." In this play the hero happens to be Jewish. One of the Arab ambassadors came to see the play in London, and warned all the other Arab embassies in London, "Howard is a dangerous Zionist. Don't go to his play." Most of them came anyway!

Q. What is your attitude towards organized labor?

A. We stand strongly in favor of trade unionism. I wish the whole world were properly united and the workers unionized. I wish the unions themselves were united.

I rejoice at the prosperity of the American unions. I thank God for the conditions you have achieved. I know the struggle you have had. But I beg you all by the mercy of God, don't forget the people who don't have unions. Don't forget the people who are still oppressed. Don't forget the people who this day as we sit here are going to bed hungry, and waking up tomorrow without hope. If we in the free world forget these people for one instant, the world we create is going to be destroyed.

Q. Do you regard Communism as the main obstacle to the moral re-armament of the world?

A. Let me be perfectly clear that Moral Re-Armament is not merely a bulwark against Communism. If Communism were to vanish off the face of the earth so no man had ever heard of it, the work of myself and my friends would remain precisely the same.

God alone knows whether the Communists in their millions, who are taught to disbelieve in a Creator, but who strive to build a heaven on earth, are more guilty than the millions of non-Communists who profess a faith but live in such a way that millions on earth are condemned to live in the hell of malnutrition, bad housing and lack of any decent upbringing or environment.

There are two theories about Communism which seem to me to be nonsense. The first is that Communism is the big Red Devil of the world. People seem to think that Communism causes broken homes, corrupt politicians, strikes and lock-outs, racial prejudice—indeed almost everything on earth including corns and cancer. I do not share the view that Communism is the big Red Devil. I think Communism is caused when a need in the human heart as well as a need in the human body remains unmet. So long as free men fail to meet these needs of flesh and spirit, Communism or the Hitlerism that attempts to put down Communism by force and brutality, will continue to march upon the earth. Communism is caused by the social and economic injustices which for too long have been permitted to exist in our free societies. It is caused by selfishness and it breeds hate.

The second theory about Communism is that here is the big Red Angel of the earth. This seems to me equally foolish and dangerous. Yet many intellectuals and people of professional skill condone or justify Communism. Sometimes I think it is to satisfy a sense of guilt in their heart that they have advantages which are denied to so many of their fellow men. They live bourgeois lives but make themselves feel more comfortable by preaching and praising the philosophy of Karl Marx.

The truth is that Communism is neither the big Red Devil nor the big Red Angel of our times. It is a symptom of a sickness that will inevitably enslave or destroy humanity unless we cure its causes. The only intelligent action for modern man seems to me to be an attempt to create the right revolution in the modern world which is big enough to include Communist and non-Communist and powerful enough to cure the hatred of class against class, race against race, color against color as well as the selfishness that causes it.

Q. Will freedom or Communism win the world?

A. Communism is going to shift the world unless we shift it first. There is only one answer to the challenge of Lenin when he said, "We shall never succeed until the myth of God is removed from the mind of man." That is an all-out effort to build man once again in the image of God. I am not talking about becoming saints. I am talking about a revolutionary aim.

What are we all living for? If it is just to use a revolution to safeguard our own property, our own position and our own lives, that revolution is bound to fail. If we are willing to sacrifice our selfishness and risk our property, our lives, our status, to serve the nation and change history, we are bound to win.

Q. What should America's role be in the world?

A. Some nation soon is going to teach the world that free men can accept an aim for humanity bigger than that of any Marxist or any Fascist. They are going to show that free men have the

109

discipline, tradition and faith to pursue that aim with passion and unanimity until it is achieved. One nation guided by God will show the world how to live. One nation at peace within itself will give the secret of peace to all nations. Such a nation will make a mark on history far beyond anything made by the French Revolution, the Russian Revolution or any revolution of materialism. And the children of the earth and their children's children will rise up and call that nation blessed.

PART THREE

Documents

The rest of this book consists of source materials selected for three reasons:

1. To answer authoritatively some lies and rumors about Moral Re-Armament.
2. To document its development in its earlier years.
3. To describe more fully its program and aims in the words of three of the men who have been responsible for its growth.

LIES AND THE TRUTH

— 1 —

A GESTAPO REPORT

A Gestapo Report, Die Oxfordgruppenbewegung, was published in 1942 by the Headquarters of the Reich Security Department of Hitler's Germany. The discovery during the German retreat from France of this 126-page document (see photo of front cover in photo section later) was first reprinted in an Associated Press dispatch by De Witt Mackenzie:

LONDON, December 19, 1945 (AP) — Ever since my tour of Germany at the time of the fateful Munich conference in 1938, I have repeatedly insisted that Adolf Hitler deliberately set about to destroy Christianity in the Fatherland, substituting the pagan creed under which he himself was a messiah, because he realized that no Christian would support his plot of murder and enslavement in Europe.

Concrete evidence that this was indeed the Nazi anti-Christ's program has now been placed in my hands here in London. This is in the form of an amazing secret report recently discovered in the files of the Reich Security Department in Berlin. Intended for official guidance, the report analyzed the operations of the Oxford Group movement (Moral Re-Armament) under the leadership of Dr. Frank Buchman, and warned that it was an instrument of Christianity, dangerous to Nazidom. The official files in Berlin also disclosed that directives for the suppression of the Oxford Group in both Germany and the occupied countries were issued on the strength of this document.

To destroy the Cross

"The Oxford Group," says the document, "as a whole constitutes an attack upon the nationalism of the State, and demands the utmost watchfulness on the part of the State. It preaches revolution against the national State and has quite evidently become its Christian opponent."

Finally, in one brutally blunt line, it discloses der Fuehrer's purpose to smash Christianity in Germany: "They (the Oxford Group) encourage their members to place themselves fully beneath the Christian Cross, and to oppose the cross of the Swastika with the Cross of Christ, as the former (the Swastika) seeks to destroy the Cross of Christ."

Sees link to diplomacy

The report reveals that the secret police regarded the Oxford Group as a force working "to bring about new political and ideological conditions in the Reich . . . At the very moment we (Nazi officialdom) are making efforts to suppress the Christian conviction of sin, which is regarded as the first step toward the enslavement of the Germans, a movement is emanating from the Anglo-Saxons, who are racially related to us, which regards just that consciousness of sin as a basis for a change in personal and national relationships."

The document stresses the bond between democracy and Christianity, and says that "the Oxford Group supplies the Christian religious garment for world democratic aims." It adds: "The group and the democracies supplement each other and render each other's work fruitful. They face the common enemy, that is, all nationalistic conceptions of life which democracy opposes and fights because of its political ideology, the Oxford Group opposes because of its primitive Christian arguments. Their common opposition to the modern conception of race and nation has brought them still closer together."

The work of the Oxford Group in other countries, including America and Britain, is dealt with, and the document sums up group activities in this fashion: "Seldom has any movement of religious rebirth succeeded as the group has in establishing itself in such a relatively short time in almost all the countries of the world . . . Under the slogan of Moral Re-Armament the group has become the pacemaker of Anglo-American diplomacy. The anti-German character of the brotherhood of the Western democracies comes out clearly in the whole propaganda for the slogan, which has the delighted support of all the Jewish propagandists of world democracy."

2

BUCHMAN AT PRINCETON

*A letter from U.S. Senator H. Alexander Smith
published in the* Princeton Alumni Weekly,
September 22 1961.

Dear Sirs:

In your issue of June 2, 1961, there appeared an essay by Professor Walter (Buzzer) Hall entitled "Early Days under Jack Hibben." I was especially interested in this essay because for many years during the twenties I was Executive Secretary of the University and closely associated with President Hibben.

There was one section of this essay, however, entitled "Buchmanite Evangelism" which I feel for the record and in justice to all parties concerned should be clarified. This is especially important now because of the death on August 9th last of Dr. Buchman in Germany. Dr. Buchman's death has caused wide publicity throughout the world regarding Moral Re-Armament which was the designation of his work during his later years.

When rumors mentioned by Professor Hall against so-called "Buchmanism" were circulated on the Princeton Campus in 1925 and 1926, President Hibben appointed a Committee to examine the facts. The work done by this Committee took place over a period of weeks during which a thorough study was made. This study was chiefly concerned with the Philadelphian Society, the undergraduate Christian organization of that time which was under the direction of graduates of Princeton who were associates of Dr. Buchman.

The unanimous report of this Committee to President Hibben was issued on December 31, 1926. Its principal conclusions are summarized in the following quotes:

"We have endeavored in every way to secure any evidence which would tend to substantiate or justify these charges . . . no evidence has been produced before us which substantiates or justifies them . . .

"Under these circumstances we feel that in justice to the General Secretary (of the Philadelphian Society) and his associates we should state that in our opinion the charges against them are in no way justified and are the result either of misapprehension or criticism without foundation.

"On the other hand, judged by results, the General Secretary's work with the Society has been carried on with signal success. . . . He has given to Princeton a reputation for efficient and fruitful Christian endeavor which is certainly not exceeded at this time by similar work carried on in any other institution . . . We think it most unfortunate that charges of such a character based upon so little evidence should have been so widely circulated."

The members of the Committee which made this study and signed the Report were:

For the Board of Trustees: Edward D. Duffield, Chairman, M.W. Jacobus, Henry J. Cochran.

For the Faculty and Administration: Christian

116

Causs, William Gillespie, John Colt, H. Alexander Smith, Secretary.

For the Board of Directors of the Philadelphian Society: John McDowell.

As the only survivor of this group and Secretary of the Committee, I feel it incumbent upon me to clarify these facts.

I recommend to all Alumni interested in the matter a careful reading of the full report of President Hibben's Committee.

(Signed) Senator H. Alexander Smith '01

Princeton, N.J.

3

AN IDEA TO WIN THE WORLD

An advertisement in Time *magazine, January 9, 1956, giving a factual account of MRA's "Statesmen's Mission" to Asia the previous summer:*

A Statesmanship that Works

The free world must boldly face the truth. Its living, thinking, planning, aims and motives are sincerely inadequate for the crisis that confronts humanity. They just do not do what needs to be done.

The Geneva Conference fails. Russia explodes an H-bomb. Germany remains divided. Asia is bewitched, the Middle East beset and the West bewildered by Soviet diplomacy's new look. What is needed is a statesmanship that works.

For all men everywhere

Here is a story America has never been told. It could decide the future.

Thirty-five years ago one man from Pennsylvania started out to remake nations by remaking men.

One experienced diplomat says: "Frank Buchman has done three things.

"*First,* he saw the need. He realized that the world was not just at the end of a great war, but at the start of the breakdown of civilization.

118

"Second, he did not stop at diagnosis. He forged an answer — an answer that works.

"Finally, he created a world force of men and women of every color, race, class and nation who have learned and lived something more than revival. They have begun a renaissance of free men — built on the experience that adequate, accurate, definite information can come from the Mind of God to the mind of man — that when man listens, God speaks — when man obeys, God acts — when men change, nations change. They have united under God to remake the world."

MRA world mission

MRA has set off a chain reaction that is spreading to the four corners of the globe. In June, 1955, 192 people from 28 countries set out from Washington on a unique ideological mission — commended by the Speaker and the Majority and Minority Leaders of the U.S. House of Representatives. They went on the invitation of heads of state and national leaders to 16 countries of Asia, the Middle East and Africa. They took with them the cast and equipment of a full-scale musical play, "The Vanishing Island," dramatizing the central struggle of our time. They traveled in U.S. Air Force planes. MRA holds the receipt for $124,930 for the cost of the planes at a rate determined by the Secretary of the Air Force to be sufficient to cover costs attributable to this trip including crew per diem, gas and oil, aircraft attrition and maintenance en route. The money came from world-wide contributions. The story of this mission is told in Peter Howard's new book, "An Idea to Win the World." For full facts about the planes see page 43 of the book. (Arrowhead Books, Inc., New York; Blandford Press, London.)

Statesmen speak

Response from the countries visited was electric.

Prime Minister Hatoyama of Japan called their visit "the most memorable experience of my life . . . a practical way to unite East and West."

Generalissimo Chiang Kai-shek: "This is the most important form of aid we have ever received."

President Ngo Dinh Diem of Vietnam: "I understand the immense repercussions that will come from this mobilization of spiritual forces."

Premier Pibulsongram of Thailand: "The peace-loving people of the world will sooner or later yield to the ideology of Moral Re-Armament. It is a strong force that answers world materialism."

The Prime Minister of Iran, Hussein Ala, following the recent attempt on his life, said: "This new lease of life will be used for continued effort to serve Iran and extend Moral Re-Armament."

Fadhil Jamali of Iraq, former Premier: "We absolutely cannot hold back from accepting this ideology presented by Moral Re-Armament."

The Tolon Na, who represents one and a half million in the Moslem north of the Gold Coast: "What Abraham Lincoln did for America, Moral Re-Armament is doing for Africa."

"The Vanishing Island"

Typical of the press response:

Nippon Times: "This event is as significant in our cultural history as the time Japan's doors were opened to modern civilization. The most appealing factor of the play was the atmosphere of purity."

Ceylon Observer: "This play portrays the germ of democracy so compellingly that millions will follow the lead of the nation that takes it to heart."

Amrita Bazar Patrika of Calcutta: "The play depicts an answer to the very problems faced by the 'Summit' Conference."

Images of Cairo: "In Cairo, where it was invited by Prime Minister Nasser, its success has been brilliant. Symbolizing a new dimension in international relations, it has made an indelible impression on the capital."

Europe responds

During the Foreign Ministers Conference, the MRA mission was in Geneva. There the influential *Journal de Geneve* devoted a four-page special supplement evaluating "its successfully undertaken mission to the capitals of Asia."

Meanwhile, the Mission is moving through Europe 350-strong. In Finland it was welcomed by President Paasikivi and by 14 bishops of Scandinavia. It went on to Kiruna, strategic source of Europe's iron ore, where Communists until the coming of MRA had controlled the works councils. Then to Stockholm, where the King and Queen of Sweden attended the play's premier. From Stockholm the Mission continued on to Oslo and Copenhagen.

Edwin Gooch, chairman of the British Labor Party, cabled to the Norwegian Labor Movement: "MRA is breaking down barriers of division over the world and establishing the basis for permanent peace."

Such is the response that the press of Scandinavia has already devoted 600 column-feet in five weeks' time.

Moscow

Moscow saw clearly the significance of MRA. Moving swiftly into the battle for men's minds in Africa, India and the Middle East, Russia repeatedly attacked MRA and warned that "It attempts to substitute for the inevitable class war the ancient struggle between good and evil . . . contaminating the minds of the masses . . . a global ideology with bridgeheads in every nation, in its final phase of total expansion throughout the world . . . has the power to capture radical revolutionary minds."

Moral Re-Armament

The calamity would be if America did not realize the full significance of this evidence until it was too late.

The free world's weakness has been the lack of a fighting faith greater than Communism. We have it in our heritage but we have not lived it in our lives. Our pronouncements to the world of how good we are, how successful we are, how comfortable we are, fail to convince the uncommitted millions of Asia and Africa and the committed world of Communism.

MRA is for everyone everywhere. It is not an organization. It is an ideology which bids effectively to change the thinking and living of nations and of the leaders of nations — before it is too late.

Admiral Richard E. Byrd, leaving recently for the Antarctic on Operation Deepfreeze, said, "There is on the march today a force that can unite men of all colors and races to answer the divisive force of materialism. I refer to Moral Re-Armament . . . it is a fight which should fire the hearts of all red-blooded Americans and stir their wills to action."

4

MRA HAS NEVER BEEN PACIFIST

Admiral William H. Standley, Former Chief of Naval Operations and Former U.S. Ambassador to Moscow, released a statement to the press from San Diego, California, March 1959:

"I have known Moral Re-Armament for 20 years. I know it is effectively answering Communism. Moscow attacks it for that reason . . . With Moral Re-Armament America can go on the offensive in the world war of ideas . . . To set the record straight, Moral Re-Armament is not and has never been pacifist. It shares equally in importance with material re-armament. Moral Re-Armament ranks with the highest form of patriotism and is providing an irreplaceable national service."

5

CATHOLICS AND MRA

The Most Reverend Thomas L. Noa, Bishop of Marquette, Michigan, wrote in Our Sunday Visitor, *the National Catholic Ecumenical Weekly, October 23, 1966, with regard to a directive he had issued in 1958 restricting Catholic participation in Moral Re-Armament:*

"In view of the decrees and declarations of the Ecumenical Council about our relations with Christians and non-Christians, I feel we should emphasize the need of supporting a movement which stands for Christian and moral principles, as does Moral Re-Armament. We think this is necessary especially in the field of education.

"The writer of this letter, as Bishop of Marquette, would today issue a directive about Catholic involvement with Moral Re-Armament revised from the directive which was issued in 1958."

On November, 1966, Our Sunday Visitor declared in its Questions and Answers column:

"May Catholics have anything to do with the movement known as Moral Re-Armament?

"Since the Second Vatican Council it is quite evident that they may and should support this movement which stands for Christian and moral principles."

On New Year's Day, 1967, Archbishop James P. Davis of Santa Fe celebrated a Mass for all those attending the Moral Re-Armament Demonstration in that city. In the course of his sermon the Archbishop said:

"Our friends in MRA are building on the truth and there are some great truths in it. One of these which I appreciate is their conviction that today belongs to anyone who wants to live it all-out and he cannot live it aloof and by himself.

"This is the strength of MRA: That we get our sights on the truths of God, on honesty and purity and pursue them not apart on our own, but with others. In this way we pursue a radical, personal vocation. Christ said, 'Be ye perfect as your Father in Heaven is perfect.' Try it and you will be surprised how much closer you can come to perfection."

IN WAR AND PEACE

— 1 —

THE GOLDEN AGE

A pamphlet outlining the aims of Moral Re-Armament widely distributed at the time of its launching in the United States, June 1939:

Three great tasks confront this generation: to keep the peace and make it permanent; to make the wealth and work of the world available to all and for the exploitation of none; and with peace and prosperity as our servants and not our masters, to build a new world, create a new culture and bring in the Golden Age.

Men have always dreamed of a Golden Age — in the future or distant past — in which all would be happy. Often they have believed that they could achieve it by their own efforts. But man's wisdom has proved wanting. Today we are at our wit's end.

Moral Re-Armament — MRA — is God's supreme offer to this generation. We in this generation may bring in the Golden Age, the new civilization built here and now on enduring foundations. It will come not by our own wisdom, but by an obedient cooperation with God in the task of Moral Re-Armament.

It will be an age of happy homes and laughing children, an age from which fear has been lifted like the smoke-pall from an industrial city, when we shall look for care-worn faces and find ncne.

It will be an age in which mothers will not fear that the children they are rearing will be killed in the next war, and husbands will not fear that next week there may be no pay envelope for them to take home to their wives.

It will be an age of peace, lasting peace in heart, home and between nations — a peace which will be not alone the absence of war, but the liberation of all our energies to build a new world.

It will be a world from which the drab misery of poverty and unemployment will be wiped away.

It will be a world in which art, literature and music will blossom into new life; where inventive genius, no longer clouded by selfishness and fear, will rise to new heights of constructive greatness.

It will be a world where youth loses its disillusion and becomes the moral backbone as well as the nerve and sinew of every nation.

A world in which society has no enemies because society makes no enemies.

A fear-free, hate-free, greed-free world.

A world in which employer and employee, city worker and farmer, doctor and teacher, will work together under God's direction to bring health and plenty, wisdom and leisure, within the reach of all.

A world in which we can be trusted with peace because it will not make us soft; with prosperity because it will not make us proud; with liberty because it will not lead to license; with happiness because it will not make us selfish.

A world in which the humblest citizen and the mightiest nation shall achieve the greatness which consists in making our greatest contribution to all.

Have we the right to dream these dreams? We have the right to dream them if we have the will to make them real.

MRA points the way. It is God's answer for this generation.

It is on the way. It is within our grasp. It must come.

The Golden Age, the new civilization can dawn in myself today, in my home tonight, and in the place where I work, tomorrow. It can dawn in my country when all who read this begin to re-arm morally, and in the world when my nation is ready to give a lead.

For thousands who have tried it, the world over, it has already begun.

For them it has made all things new.

It will mean self-sacrifice? So did the last war; so would the next. The self-sacrifice of this generation in the cause of MRA will mean the salvation of the next.

The battle for peace is being fought here and now. It is being fought each day in your heart and will.

Who knows how quickly the issue can be decided if you re-arm morally and enter the fray?

2

LAUNCHING MORAL
RE-ARMAMENT IN AMERICA

Extract from the Congressional Record, June 8, 1939. Speech of Harry S. Truman of Missouri in the Senate of the United States:

MR. TRUMAN. Mr. President, on Sunday, June 4, there was held in Constitution Hall, Washington, the National Meeting for Moral Re-Armament. I had the honor at that time to present the following message from the President of the United States, which opened that great assembly:

"The underlying strength of the world must consist in the moral fiber of her citizens. A program of moral re-armament for the world cannot fail, therefore, to lessen the danger of armed conflict. Such moral re-armament, to be most highly effective, must receive support on a world-wide basis."

Franklin D. Roosevelt

That meeting was sponsored by members of the Cabinet and Members of the Senate and House of Representatives, and the invitation to the meeting contained messages from the Secretary of State, the Secretary of War, the Attorney-General, the Speaker of the House, the leader of the Senate majority, former President Hoover, the Senator from Kansas (Mr. Capper), the Senator from New York

(Mr. Wagner), Hon. Joseph W. Martin, Jr., the minority leader in the House of Representatives. There was also one from John J. Pershing, General of the Armies of the United States in the last war.

The principal address of the evening was delivered by Dr. Frank N. D. Buchman, founder of the Oxford Group. There were messages from the House of Lords of Great Britain signed by twenty-five members of that body, and a message from the House of Commons signed by two hundred and forty members of that body.

I think it is particularly appropriate, Mr. President, to record these messages from Great Britain in the proceedings of the Senate today because of the presence here of the King and Queen of Great Britain, and because of the fact that included among the signatories are men who both personally and officially are associated with Their Majesties.

From Members of the House of Lords:

"We, being members of the House of Lords in Great Britain, wish to congratulate you at the great meeting to promote moral and spiritual re-armament, which is about to take place in Washington. Unity and peace, whether national or international, can grow only amongst men and nations who become spiritually equipped with faith and love. The responsibility before God rests upon every individual man and woman, with us and with you, that they answer to this call.

From Members of the House of Commons:

"We, the undersigned members of the British House of Commons, send greetings on the occasion of the national meeting for moral re-armament in Washington. We join you in affirming our loyalty to those moral and spiritual principles which are more fundamental than any political or economic issue and which are the common heritage of our peoples.

"Only if founded on moral and spiritual re-armament can democracy fulfil its promise to mankind and perform its part in creating a mutual understanding between nations and restoring peace to the world.

Then follow messages from representatives of British Labor, Industry and Commerce and from members of the Netherlands Cabinet, from representatives of the Swiss, Danish, Finnish, Norwegian and Swedish Parliaments; and from leaders in France, Turkey and the Balkans. Senator Truman summed up the occasion with these words:

May I say again, Mr. President, how fitting it is to record these messages from Great Britain in view of the great welcome which the Nation's capital has just given the King and Queen, and of the fact that moral re-armament is strengthening those spiritual qualities which are the common heritage of our peoples, and the strongest bond between us.

It is rare in these days, Mr. President, to find something which will unite men and nations on a plane above conflict of party, class, or political philosophy. I am sure that I voice the sentiment of all of us here today in expressing gratification at a response so remarkable to a need so urgent, and confidence that America will play her full part in this cause on whose fortunes the future of civilization must largely depend.

3

YOU CAN DEFEND AMERICA

Moral Re-Armament published a wartime hand-
book in 1941 with a foreword by General of the
Armies John J. Pershing. Following is the text:

FOREWORD
by
The General of the Armies
of the United States of America

This little book is aptly titled "You Can Defend America." No patriotic citizen can read it without feeling its inspiration. None can fail fully to indorse its ultimate objective — the preservation of our precious heritage. It invokes the principles of good citizenship and the spirit of '76 and '17 in this new emergency confronting our great democracy. How each of us can do his part in the home, in industry, in every walk of life, is indicated clearly and forcefully. I commend its message to every American.

(Signed) *John J. Pershing*

ONCE CHINA BUILT A WALL

She lived behind it. She laughed at her enemies. She felt secure.

Soon an invader came from the north. Three times China found the enemy inside her gates. They did not storm the wall. They did not go around it. They simply bribed the gate-keepers.

YESTERDAY FRANCE BUILT A WALL

The Maginot Line. Steel and stone. She felt secure behind it. She put her faith in it.

Yet France fell. Why?

Something was missing. There was a gap through which an invader came. That gap was not only in the wall. It was in the spirit of the people.

TODAY AMERICA BUILDS A WALL

A ring of steel. Ships and planes and guns.

But is this enough?

Does America have what China lacked? What France lacked? Does she have *total* defense?

She builds her wall. Does she build character? Spirit? The will to sacrifice?

Does she build men? Men who pull together?

Before our eyes the world changes. Nations collapse.

We in America ask: "What can I do?" What can 130 million Americans do? PLENTY!

Behind ships, planes and guns stand three lines of defense:

SOUND HOMES

TEAMWORK IN INDUSTRY

A UNITED NATION

They fill the gap—they must be manned

SOUND HOMES—The First Line of Defense

Why don't the nations get along like one big family? A humorist answers, "The trouble is they do!"

Homes are the cement of national life. The place where the nation learns how to live together. The non-stop assembly line of character which is the heart of national morale. If homes crack, the nation cracks.

Family life once made America great. Home building was an art. But it went out with the horse and buggy. For millions today home means only a filling station by day and a parking place at night. Divorce is rapidly becoming part of the American Way. And the birth-rate continues to go down.

Many of us would willingly die for our family, but sometimes find it pretty tough having to live with them. So Father pays the bills. Mother worries. The children do as they please. We like to sing "Home Sweet Home" — when we're away from home.

To defend America we need sound homes. Where the family hide nothing from one another and help one another to give their best. Where there is plenty of laughter and love. Where meals are not just gulp and go, but where the company and conversation are as good as the food. Where the welcome sign is always out. Where neighbors can drop in to borrow a cup of flour and find real friendship. And courage when times are hard.

Homes that pull together pull the town together. And unite the nation.

Fathers who know how to unite their families will take that spirit into their jobs. If they can settle private strikes and lockouts at home, they know the way to industrial cooperation.

Mothers who teach their children responsibility, faith and discipline will build the nation's character.

Families who allow no waste in their kitchens will show the nation how to use all of everything. Their thrift will help make America secure.

Sound homes will produce not only the manpower, but the will power to defend America.

TEAMWORK IN INDUSTRY—The Second Line of Defense

War in industry has cost Americans $3,000,000 a day. It can sabotage any re-armament program. It can cripple a nation before an army gets into the field.

France failed in the factory before she failed at the front. Her people forgot how to pull together. Employers refused to sacrifice. Men refused to work. In her zero hour desperation was no substitute for preparation. She was lost.

America must win the battle for industrial cooperation if she is to be secure. Every man has a part. Every worker, every employer, every labor leader.

"If we perspired more in time of peace, we would bleed less in time of war," said Generalissimo Chiang Kai-shek.

Americans know how to work. We must work harder. Not every man for himself, but every man for his country, whatever his job.

We must work with all we've got. America is like a car hitting on half its cylinders — and there is a steep hill ahead. Much of her power is wasted. Waste in the factory, waste on the land. Waste of time, waste of money, waste of men.

We must work together. Friction between men slows up work more than friction in machines. If employers or workers destroy teamwork by their selfishness, then America is in danger. And the gains each fought for will be swept away.

The defense of the nation demands that all rise above self-interest. It means each faces up to his own mistakes. It means we join forces for the common good.

Then our industries will run at capacity. Our man power will be put to work. Together we all will produce the materials and morale to make America strong.

A UNITED NATION—The Third Line of Defense

America does not need to be divided and quarreling at home just to prove she is a democracy — any more than husband and wife need to get into an argument just to prove they have minds of their own.

A crack football team isn't all made up of quarterbacks. Every man has his part. Each depends on all the others. So with the nation. Unless we have national teamwork someone is likely to take the ball away from us.

Nations in Europe have gone down because they were at war inside themselves. Their people couldn't get together. They refused to face facts. They were caught unprepared. Even as the storm broke, men fought to get more for themselves.

National unity is the heart of national defense. If a nation is united, no Fifth Column can slip through and sabotage its strength.

A united people will have the spirit which no disaster will shake and no danger will weaken.

Unity is more than agreeing on what we like or whom we hate. Teamwork cannot be built by high talking and low living; by fine ideals and selfish lives.

"Teamwork," said Knute Rockne, "is a combination of self-sacrifice, brains and sweat." It means working together for America. Honest teamwork between government and business, labor and management, union and union, republican and democrat, city and farm.

A united people will build the new America. A nation set free from fear, hate and greed. A nation that holds the secret of the new world.

WHAT YOU CAN DO

America needs guts as well as guns
National character is the core of national defense

CONGRESS CAN'T VOTE IT
DOLLARS WON'T BUY IT
IT'S YOUR JOB TO BUILD IT

How? CHANGE! UNITE! FIGHT!

CHANGE!

Human nature is the bottleneck in the production of national morale. We need a new spirit in the country. But to get it we must start with a new spirit in every citizen. And that means *you*.

Either you sacrifice your personal selfishness for the nation — or you sacrifice the nation for your personal selfishness.

America needs a change of heart. We must *live* the American Way.

Americans are honest, unselfish, neighborly, clean and free.

Or are they? Always? Are you? All the time? If not, what can you do about it?

A new spirit can grip your heart and mind and muscle — if you are willing. You can change. How?

The first step is to face the facts. The facts about yourself. Honest? Unselfish? Neighborly? Clean? Free? At home? In industry? In politics?

Our fathers looked to God for their direction. We've looked about every place else.

We still print "In God We Trust" on our money. Everybody carries the idea around in his pocket. Is it just an idea? Or is it the main point?

William Penn said, "Men must be governed by God, or they will be ruled by tyrants."

What are you governed by? Your wife? Your husband? Your desires? Your pocketbook? Fear of losing your job? Personal ambition?

Only God can change human nature. When you decide to be governed by God, then the change comes.

It's like joining the army. You decide there's something worth fighting for. You enlist. You put yourself under orders. Then you are given new equipment. You find new comradeship. Your way of living changes. And your whole outlook on life.

To be governed by God means to listen to a Wisdom beyond your own. And obey.

George Washington listened at a time of conflict — and gave a nation freedom.

Abraham Lincoln listened at a time of crisis — and preserved a nation's unity.

Lincoln said, "I have so many evidences of God's direction that I cannot doubt this power comes from above. I am satisfied that when the Almighty wants me to do or not to do any particular thing, He finds a way of letting me know it."

You don't have to be President to do as Lincoln did. When you take time to be quiet and listen, God will guide your thoughts. He will give you orders. And a plan. Directions how to put things right. Creative ideas about yourself, your home, your job, your community, your nation. How you can strengthen America's three lines of defense.

Make a note of the thoughts you get. Test them. Are they honest? Unselfish? Neighborly? Clean? Then put them to work.

As you act on them you will begin to change. So will your home and your community. The Land of the Free will be the home of the strong, and the spirit of our people invincible.

. . . "That this nation, under God, shall have a new birth of freedom" . . .

UNITE!

When you find the secret of change and getting direction from God, you can play your full part in a program of total defense.

You can overcome disunity wherever you find it. You will be a rallying point for all citizens who want to do their bit. Your home will be a recruiting center. Your neighborhood a sample of the new America — the America where democracy works.

Such national unity doesn't just happen. It begins with you and the fellow you don't get along with.

If you start changing, the other fellow will sit up and take notice. If you put things straight with him, maybe he'll put things straight with you.

Everybody wants to see the other fellow different. But everybody is waiting for the other fellow to begin. The secret of national unity is to have the guts to begin with yourself.

Honest apology starts teamwork.

Try it at home. Thousands of families are making the experiment. Mrs. Jones who was "always right" apologizes. Mr. Jones decides to be honest too. The children say, "Gee, it's fun to be home now!" The neighbors keep up with the Joneses — in bringing a new spirit to their families. Backyard gossip changes to planning for the community. Planning for sound homes. Planning to defend America.

If boss and worker put *all* their cards on the table, in this spirit of honest apology, would strikes and lockouts be necessary? Or would we have teamwork in industry?

If political parties admitted where they'd been at fault, there'd be less mud-slinging and more of the honesty that builds a nation. There'd be more of a common loyalty to America, above party, class, race, point of view, and personal advantage.

That's not just the job of the politicians; or of management; or of labor. It is *yours*.

It is your job to work to make this country you love into One All-American Team.

FIGHT!

Musket and powder-horn once hung over the door of every American home. Our fathers were not afraid to use them. The Minute Men at Lexington and Concord seized them and ran to defend their country. Not a man in America would hesitate to do it again if invaders threatened his homeland.

But America has already been invaded. Like parachute troops in the night, fear, hate and greed have slipped into our homes, our industries, our communities. Like termites they are eating away our national character.

The fight is on. The fight against our softness, graft, laziness, extravagance, buckpassing, materialism — allies of the Fifth Column. The battle line runs through every home, every office, every factory, every farm.

It is a daily battle. It takes courage. Imagination. You've got to be tough inside. You've got to think hard, and live clean.

You and 130 million other Americans can enlist today in this fight. You don't have to wait to be put into uniform. You're in the army now.

First lick the enemy inside yourself. Then get the next fellow to join you in this battle for a new America. Get your newspaper, radio station and movie theater to fight for a new morale.

Fight to make your home and community a pattern.

Fight to bring teamwork in industry.

Fight to unite the nation.

Then America will have what ancient China lacked. What modern France lacked. She will have *total defense*.

AMERICA—This land of towering cities and golden prairies, of great rivers and mighty mountains. This nation of Washington and Jefferson, of Lincoln and Lee and Edison, and countless thousands of ordinary men and women, who crossed oceans and plains, who toiled long for little reward, who sacrified and built our heritage.

If that heritage was worth their lives to build, it is worth ours to preserve.

"And in support of this declaration, with a firm reliance on the protection of Divine Providence, we mutually pledge to each other our lives, our fortunes and our sacred honor."

4

THE WAR-TIME PROGRAM
OF MRA

The Army and Navy Journal *of Washington, D.C.,
published the following, May 6, 1944:*

'Napoleon's axiom, "Morale is to material as three is to one" has been upset. The ratio now stands at six to one.' This statement of General Marshall's takes on new importance as we make preparations to strike with an invasion force. Our leaders know that to the excellence of arms and training must be added the decisive weapons of heart, mind and will to absorb the shock of battle and carry through to victory.

An important factor in building this fighting spirit on both battlefront and home front has been the program of Moral Re-Armament. In a report recently published here, a group of British leaders, political, industrial and military, write: 'National strength springs from the spirit of the people. In time of war that spirit is decisive, and it will be no less needed in the years after victory. For this reason, we, with large numbers of representative citizens in this country recognize the vital importance of the work for Moral Re-Armament and believe that they should be given every encouragement in their essential national service. Their wo has proved its success in bringing to life for n and women of all classes the great spiritual values which are the fabric of our nation and for which we battle.'

The MRA program was outlined for America eight months before Pearl Harbor in terms of sound homes, teamwork in industry and national unity, in a widely read handbook entitled *You Can Defend America*, with a foreword by General Pershing. This was dramatized in a war revue of the same name which in the next year and a half was shown before a quarter of a million people in over twenty States, and which was the spearhead of campaigns to build a war-winning spirit throughout the nation.

Since Pearl Harbor Moral Re-Armament has been credited by competent observers such as Senator Truman and Congressman Wadsworth with increasing war production in many key aircraft plants and shipyards. Senator Truman said of MRA: 'They have rendered great assistance to the all-out war program by creating the spirit of cooperation between management and labor, reducing absenteeism, heightening all-round efficiency and increasing production. There is not a single industrial bottleneck I can think of which could not be broken in a matter of weeks if this crowd were given the green light to go full steam ahead.'

Major General Francis B. Wilby, Superintendent of the U.S. Military Academy, after inspecting the results of their work on the home front, said: 'This is the arm behind the army.' Admiral Richard E. Byrd described it as 'the fight for a new America, ong, clean and united.'

Britain, which has faced invasion and blitz,

MRA has played a distinctive part in toughening the spirit of the people.

During the four and a half years of war, soldiers, sailors and airmen of the United Nations have thronged MRA's training centers in America, England, Canada and Australia. A soldier visiting the London MRA headquarters the other day said, 'MRA added a plus to my training. I knew what I was fighting against. Now I know what I am fighting for.'

In Norway and other occupied countries Moral Re-Armament has stood up as an unshakable center of resistance to the Nazi oppression. Though some of its leaders have undergone imprisonment and death, MRA remains a bulwark for a liberated Europe.

We are fighting a war not alone of arms but of ideas. The victor must be strong in both. Cutting through the selfish, soft materialism and moral confusion of the last two decades, MRA has taken the soldierly virtues of discipline, sacrifice and teamwork, of patriotism essential both in war and peace, and applied them fearlessly to home life, industrial and national life. In this battle MRA has cut across and drawn the fire of self-seeking subversive elements and rallied the constructive and patriotic forces in the defense of the nation.

5

TRANSFORMATION OF SOCIETY

Robert Schuman, while Minister of Foreign Affairs of France, wrote the foreword to the French edition of Dr. Frank Buchman's speeches, published May 1950:

The editors of these speeches have decided to entrust the writing of the preface to a man in political life, a Cabinet Minister in office. We have to admit, however, that thus far statesmen have been only moderately successful in 'remaking the world.' The fact remains that it is their duty, more than anyone else's, to apply themselves to this task; and it is to their advantage to welcome every assistance offered to them.

If we were being presented with some new scheme for the public welfare or another theory to be added to the many already put forward, I should remain sceptical. But what Moral Re-Armament brings us is a philosophy of life applied in action.

It does not claim to have invented a new system of morals. For the Christian, the moral teaching of Christianity is enough, and he draws from it all the principles which must guide his life as a man and as a citizen.

What we do need, and what is quite new, is a school where, by a process of mutual teaching, we can work out our practical behaviour towards others; a school where Christian principles are not only applied and proven in the relationships of man to man, but succeed in overcoming the prejudices and enmities which separate classes, races and nations.

To begin by creating a moral climate in which true brotherly unity can flourish, over-arching all that today tears the world apart — that is the immediate goal.

The acquisition of wisdom about men and their affairs by bringing people together in public assemblies and personal encounters — that is the means employed.

To provide teams of trained men, ready for the service of the state, apostles of reconciliation and builders of a new world, that is the beginning of a far-reaching transformation of society in which, during fifteen war-ravaged years, the first steps have already been made.

It is not a question of change of policy; it is a question of changing men. Democracy and her freedoms can be saved only by the quality of the men who speak in her name.

That is what Dr. Buchman expresses in simple and moving words. He has declared war on materialism and individualism, twin generators of our selfish divisions and social injustices.

May he be heard and followed more and more, in all nations of the world, by those who today still clash in fratricidal hatred.

RÉPUBLIQUE FRANÇAISE
LIBERTÉ - ÉGALITÉ - FRATERNITÉ

ROBERT SCHUMAN
DÉPUTÉ DE LA MOSELLE

PARIS, LE 19 Juillet 1956

Dear friend Frank Buchman,

Je vous suis très reconnaissant de votre aimable et
intéressante lettre du 28 Juin.

Je sais le bon travail que vous avez accompli, avec
vos amis, en Tunisie et au Maroc. Toutes les difficultés ne sont
pas encore résolues ; mais, vous avez su créer un climat favorable.

Je garde le souvenir très vif et reconnaissant de nos
rencontres à Caux, à Paris et ailleurs.

Avec mon très fidèle souvenir

Monsieur Frank Buchman
45 Berkeley Square
London W1

Robert Schuman, French Foreign Minister, thanks Frank Buchman for MRA's services in Tunisia and Morocco.

— 6 —

SHAPING INTERNATIONAL RELATIONS

The New York Journal-American of January 31, 1960, published an article by Dr. Konrad Adenauer, who was then Chancellor of the Federal Republic of Germany.

At this time of confusion in Europe we need, and especially in divided Germany, an ideology that brings clarity and moral power into shaping international relations. A nation with an ideology is always on the offensive. A nation without an ideology is self-satisfied and dead.

Communism has gone through many phases — Marxism, Leninism, Stalinism, and now Khrushchev. But one thing has remained unaltered — its aim of world domination. We must be prepared to continue the ideological struggle for several decades yet, but I am convinced Khrushchev's grandchildren will not be Communists.

Dr. Frank Buchman, founder of Moral Re-Armament, is making a great contribution to international unity and to the establishment of social justice. A lasting memorial to his work is established in the hearts of mankind of this age. The way he has labored to establish relationships between men and nations on firm foundations of moral values will never be forgotten.

Now is the time to work more strongly than ever for European unity through MRA. A Europe in which freedom and brotherhood should reign can only be created when nations are mutually conscious of their moral responsibility. MRA has given most valuable stimulation to the great work of uniting Europe. Unless this work is carried forward, peace in the world cannot be maintained.

If all nations are to continue to live together, one of the most pressing tasks of our age is to overcome prejudices that exist between people, races and nations. In this field MRA has made an important contribution.

May it above all pass on the truth that the one real hope of nations living together in peace can only be found through a change in the human heart.

We can be grateful to the men and women of Moral Re-Armament that in this world of destruction they have had the courage to raise the banner of moral values. MRA has become a household word in postwar Germany.

The German people gratefully recognize the help which has come so readily to them through MRA. Very soon after the end of the war this ideology reached out a hand to the German people and helped them make contact again with other nations. In Western Germany MRA has worked very forcefully in the creation of good relations between management and labor.

Men and nations cannot outwardly enjoy stable relations until they have been inwardly prepared for them. In this respect MRA has rendered great and lasting services.

We have seen the conclusion after some difficult negotiations of important international agreements.

MRA has played an invisible but effective part in bridging differences of opinion between negotiating parties. It has kept before them the objective of peaceful agreement in search for common good which is the true purpose of human life.

Begin with yourself — that, in my opinion, is the basic challenge of MRA. May this challenge ring out far and wide across the whole world and into all nations.

BUNDESREPUBLIK DEUTSCHLAND
DER BUNDESKANZLER

BONN

Rhöndorf
28. 5. 50

Chancellor Adenauer, in a handwritten letter, invites Buchman to hold an MRA demonstration in Germany.

düstern Frieden.

Möge der Ruf von Caux
weit hinausdringen in alle
Welt und unter alle Völ-
ker!

[Unterschrift]

Bundesbruder
zur Pfingst.-Bundestagung
im Jahre 1950!

FROM ONE MAN TO MILLIONS

— 1 —

REVIVAL, REVOLUTION, RENAISSANCE

Address by Frank Buchman
Visby, Sweden, August 1938

Today we want to forge a united battlefront. The clear issue is whether we are guided by God or not. It is not whether we are clever. It is not what nation we belong to. We meet here today as Christians and we meet as guided people, and our final source of authority is God's plan.

I hope that by the time I finish speaking some of you will have made a decision. We have come here with different objectives. First, some of the people have come here hoping to be changed. That is very good, very necessary. Some of you come here with the hope that you will learn to change others. That, too, is very necessary.

But the danger is that some of you want to stop there. I am tremendously interested in a third point — how to save a crumbling civilization. That is the thing that interests me. But then I want a fourth thing. I want to reach the millions of the world.

All these things ought naturally to follow each other. If you are changed, you naturally want to change other people. The next thing is you want to save civilization. Then you want to reach the millions out there. It is a natural program.

But sin comes along. I don't know if you believe in it or not, but it is here. Don't spend the rest of the day arguing if it exists or not. That is what some of you would like to do. You would miss the whole point. We are not here to argue; we are here for constructive planning and action.

I know what some of you would like out of the Oxford Group — a nice comfortable awakening; you would call it a revival. A nice armchair religion. That is the thinking of some people. But if we stopped there, I should be sorry. If you stop there, I am your enemy unless I warn you. A person who has that conception today is not adequately thinking and planning to save the millions.

I am not interested, nor do I think it adequate, if we are going to begin just to start another revival. Whatever thoughtful statesman you talk to will tell you that every country needs a moral and spiritual awakening. That is the absolutely fundamental essential. But revival is only one level of thought. To stop there is inferior thinking. Unless we call for something bigger than that we are done for.

The next step is revolution. It is uncomfortable. A lot of Christians don't like the word. It scares them. It makes them goose-fleshy. That's where some of your critics come from — goose-fleshy Christians with armchair Christianity.

Begin to work out how many still go to church and ask why the church today is not reaching one hundred per cent of the people. I know revolution makes people uncomfortable. I am not here to make you comfortable, and I am not here to make you like me. What the Oxford Group will give this and every nation is a spiritual revolution.

But some of you are not thinking this way. Some of the cleverest people in the world are thinking along the line of destructive revolution, and they are already at work. May I say a very strong word to you this morning? I find here the same sort of inflammable matter that made Spain possible. Unless we and others see the bigger vision of spiritual revolution, the other may be possible.

Think of the uncomfortableness of that kind of revolution. We are met in a ruined church. How many churches are in ruins in Spain today? That is revolution — very uncomfortable. The point is this. Are the Christians going to build a Christian philosophy that will move Europe? Are you the kind of Christians that can build that revolution? Is that the New Testament? Is that Christian? Is that the sort of thing you are going to do? Is that your program? Is that your policy?

If you are not going on that battlefront, I wish you well. I am not going to quarrel with you or criticize you. You do exactly what you like in the way you like. That's your idea of democracy.

I don't say it's true democracy, but it's the popular practice of democracy. For an increasing number of citizens in democratic states are now unwilling to acknowledge in speech and action those inner authorities on which the life of democracy depends. Each man has his own plan. It's so wonderful each to have his own plan. It's such freedom, such liberty! Everyone does as he pleases. But not in the Oxford Group. There you have true democracy. You don't do as you please, you do as God guides. You do God's plan.

I cannot go into all the qualities necessary for a revolutionary this morning. There were some people in the Acts and the Gospels who gave everything. There were others who did not give everything. Even in a revolution some people want an amount of padding around them. I want to ask you this morning whether you want to be that kind of a revolutionary. If so, there may be a comfortable place for you behind the lines. But somewhere on the battlefront we will have the real revolutionaries.

There is a third stage — renaissance. The rebirth of a people, individuals and the rebirth of a nation. I know what you may say. Illusion. Illusion. Illusion. Insanity. What is the insanity? Where is it?

I thank God tremendously for what has been done in this place, for all the preparations you have made, for all the difficulties you have overcome. Grateful for all that, but let's remember there is still sin in the camp. And that sin may be inferior thinking.

You will do well today to read the fifty-first psalm. It is a tremendous human experience. And then read in the New Testament about the Cross of Christ. You will never, never, never come into this experience until you know the Cross of Christ. Some of you have heard about it, Sunday by Sunday, but it's not an experience. If it were experience, you would not shrink from anything.

I am going to promise you one thing. I am not turning back. I am not turning back, no matter who does, no matter what it is going to cost. I do not want you to come along just because I am here — that isn't it. That would be a poor revolution. That would be a poor fellowship. Let us for a moment see a picture of the Cross of Christ, and let me say, if you join in this great crusade, you will get the way of the Cross. I am not going to lure you by hopes of material success. I am not going to lure you by saying you are going to be heroes. I am not going to lure you, although I believe that these lands can give a pattern on how to live. It is a personal experience of the Cross. It is not I, but Christ. It is not I at the head, but Christ who leads.

There are meetings this afternoon — the lawyers, the educationalists. These are important, but there is another more important. Cancel all others if you must for this one — the meeting between God and yourself. The biggest thing this afternoon for you may be to go off alone and decide whether you are going to be one of these fellow-revolutionaries, where you are going to stand on this battlefront. I am not going to ask you to make a decision right now. The thing you have got to decide is between you and God. Do it alone. Write it down if you want to. It is a deed, like the transfer of property — so you turn over your life to God, for full and complete direction as a fellow-revolutionary.

Then you are going to be free. Then you are going to have true democracy because you are free. That's my challenge to you.

— 2 —

BACKBONE OF THE
REAL AMERICA

Address by Frank Buchman
Washington, D.C., June 1939

MRA is the triumph of a God-given thought. It came as the answer to a crisis that threatened civilization. A re-emphasis of old truths was let loose in the world — simple home-spun truths that have been the backbone of the real America — the guidance of God and a change of heart.

Everyone agreed that these great truths had to be recaptured, relived and restored to authority — truths which, were they practiced, would bring the answer. The phrase that riveted itself upon the attention of men and women everywhere was "Moral and Spiritual Re-Armament."

Leadership of the future goes to the men of moral courage; the men who ask and give three feet to the yard, sixteen ounces to the pound. As Americans, as patriots, we find that MRA is the common denominator on which everyone can unite. In an age of material perfection we must usher in the age of spiritual force. The Voice of God must become the voice of the people; the Will of God the will of the people. This is the true democracy.

America is not without her problems in business,

the home, in industry, in civic and in government life. We need a re-dedication of our people to the elementary virtues of honesty, unselfishness and love; and we must have the will again to find what unites people rather than what divides them. It must become the dawn of a new era, a new age, a new civilization.

The future depends not only on what a few men may decide to do in Europe, but upon what a million men decide to be in America.

3

THE WAR OF IDEAS

Address by Frank Buchman
Mackinac Island, Michigan, July 1943

Today I want to talk about great forces at work in the world. Sixty and more years ago you didn't hear much about the Communist Party. To begin with there was one man — Karl Marx. Then for a long time only a small group. Eventually world conditions made it possible for Karl Marx to do his work — and Communism is the result.

Think what Russia means in the world today. How large is it? One-sixth of the earth. I remember a time when the Czar couldn't ride unless he had every six feet a man watching him. Even if it was a railway journey of a thousand miles, he always had men posted along the way. It was all part of what helped produce the thing called Communism.

A little while ago the world didn't think much about it. It didn't affect us. We had not come into contact with it. Occasionally there would be a flare-up. Then during the last war there was more and more discontent. There was revolution. And the Communist Party came to power.

Today the Russians are doing pretty well. America is doing a lot for them because just now they seem to be a decisive factor in dealing with Germany, and because they may have a controlling interest in the future.

Now that is one picture. Give it a nice gold frame. Put in as much red as you want. But when you have done that, you haven't done with Communism because it is a tremendous force. Think of the number of people in this country who have been swung by it, who have gone part way and are "leftist" in their thinking. We are going to meet it all the time.

Now take another force. When did we begin to hear about Fascism? 1921 — 1922. Again there was a man — Mussolini. I remember when I was in Italy, at Milan. *Vivai Communisti* was written all over the walls. Soon you saw *Viva il Duce* also on the walls — and Mussolini arose as an opposing force to Communism. He marched on Rome. He put himself in power and a Fascist force came into being. For a while there was a growing sense of stability and prosperity. People said, "Good! Mussolini has come. Fascism has come. The trains are on time. There are no beggars in the streets. We have 'good order.'"

But today where is Mussolini? Where is Italy? and where is the "order"?

In those days, back in the 'twenties,' Germany was at its lowest ebb. Many had no food — nothing. I remember men of large means taking a hard-boiled egg in their pocket and bringing it out for lunch. For years there was danger of collapse and incipient revolution. The youth were completely out of hand, delinquent, roving the country, with crimes of violence and theft everywhere.

Then along came a man called Hitler who had very definite ideas. He wrote them in a book when he was in prison. When he came out there were

159

mobs, disorders and massacres. The Austrian became a citizen of the German Reich. There was no order in Germany. But this juggernaut comes along and gives seeming order. More and more he took a place in the world. So the German people said, "Hallelujah!" and *Heil Hitler!* You know the rest of the story.

So we have Communism and Fascism, two world forces. And where do they come from? From Materialism which is the mother of all the 'isms.' It is the spirit of anti-Christ which breeds corruption, anarchy and revolution. It undermines our homes, it sets class against class, it divides the nation. Materialism is Democracy's greatest enemy.

These then were the forces which threatened to dominate the world.

In 1938 the guidance came to me — "Moral Re-Armament," a movement where the moral and spiritual would have the emphasis. The need of the age is the moral and the spiritual. Our task was to bring back these realities to nations that needed them. We initiated this thinking in London's East Ham Town Hall. We took it to the nations. MRA was born that year.

Communism and Fascism are built on a *negative* something — on divisive materialism and confusion. Wherever Moral Re-Armament goes, there springs up a *positive* message. Its aim is to restore God to leadership as the directing force in the life of the nation. Let me recall what I said in Philadelphia on my birthday:

"Moral Re-Armament creates the qualities that make democracy function. It is simple, non-partisan, non-sectarian, non-political. It gives to every man the inner discipline he needs and the inner liberty he desires. It calls out and combines the moral and spiritual responsibility of individuals for their immediate sphere of action.

"It builds for democracy an unshakeable framework of actively selfless and self-giving citizens, whose determination to bring unity cannot be altered by any beckoning of personal advantage and who know how to pass along to others their panic-proof experience of the guidance of God."

America must discover her rightful ideology. It springs from her Christian heritage and is her only adequate answer in the battle against materialism and all the other 'isms.' But America does not hate materialism. Think of America destroying herself with the very force that she condemns in others. The battle of the ideologies was the granite of the Old and New Testaments. So many people today instead of giving the granite, give the sugar — and so we never cure materialism.

MRA first of all goes straight to the fundamental problem — it recognizes sin. Sin is the disease. Jesus Christ is the cure. The result is a miracle. You come to a training center like this. You may say, "Oh, I don't like to hear sin mentioned." Well, that's too bad. It ought to be mentioned, but it ought to be enough just to give a quick picture of it and then move on. And you ought to be so sensitive that you respond immediately and change — and that's one more miracle. That ought to happen today, just as in the old days your grandparents used to go to church on Wednesday night, because they liked a good rugged sermon on sin. That's fine if you have time enough for it — and possibly you need to take time. Make sure there is no minimum emphasis on sin. Make it maximum. But then quickly make the adjustment. Change, unite, fight. That is the natural sequence.

161

You will find here the old fundamental truths — but you get them with a mighty, moving crescendo. MRA restores absolute standards in a day when selfishness and expediency are the common practice of men and nations. Take the four absolutes — honesty, purity, unselfishness, love. Perhaps some of you do not put much stock in them any more. But to arm a people you must give them these simple, basic standards.

Take honesty for a start. What do you find in the nation? What about men who have been dishonest, say in war contracts? Graft and the Black Market keep a lot of people busy all the time and cost millions of dollars. In the old days nobody said a good word for dishonesty. Now the successful chiseller seems almost at a premium.

Take purity. You may say that it is just a personal matter. But what is happening to the nation? They tell you that in some war plants impurity is so common that it is even organized among the workers, and especially among the subversive groups who use it as a weapon. They know that when people's morals are confused their thinking becomes confused. People say, "That's too bad," and keep on going to church on Sunday, but nothing happens. Too few try to bring a great cleansing force to the nation. What is going to happen to a nation when nobody brings a cure any more? Broken homes, unstable children, the decay of culture, the seeding plot of revolution.

As far as unselfishness and love go, people don't pretend to be unselfish, and they don't expect to be loving.

People have written off the four standards as part of the horse-and-buggy days. So, naturally, they are the last thing they have in mind for nations. That is why you have the condition there is in the world today. Now if you can get people who will live up to these absolutes and stand for them, then you have a force, a creative something in the community with a strength that nothing will gainsay.

You must have that emphasis on morals plus the saving power of Jesus Christ. Then you experience the dynamic which is almost forgotten — the Holy Spirit, that gives the guided answer and tells you exactly what to do as a clear direct call from God.

That's the program for the Church today. I believe with all my heart in the Church, the Church aflame, on fire with revolution. We haven't begun to experience the spiritual revolution we need. You need revolution, and then when you come into the clear light of God's Presence, you will experience a glorious renaissance. You will come to see what Christ means this old world to be.

It's one thing to know these realities. But there's a further thing, and that is to make them national.

The trouble with some of you is that you are so idealistic that your hopes never come to pass, even in your own families. That was the trouble with the League of Nations. People were so "League-minded" they failed to do the thing the League most needed — the spadework with individuals that brings change. There was something left out of the League and that was — God. The League was never God-arched.

Everybody's job is to find the God-arched master-plan. Then we would have a master-plan not only for us, but for post-war Europe. The trouble is, we let the statesmen do all our thinking for us — and then we call it democracy!

Take the great modern cities you come from.

163

You complain of this subversive leader and that one. Yet it is the selfishness of everyone that makes possible the subversive leader. The whole problem is that you endure a thing rather than cure it. You would rather pay than pray. You would rather go on with your confusion, your grumbling, your complaints, than change and have an answer.

The battle for America is the battle for the mind of America. A nation's thinking is in ruins before a nation is in ruins. And America's thinking is in ruins.

People get confused as to whether it is a question of being Rightist or Leftist. But the one thing we really need is to be guided by God's Holy Spirit. That is the Force we ought to study. Then we will have a clear light that ends confusion. The Holy Spirit will teach us how to think and live, and provide a working basis for our national service.

America doesn't have much of her great moral heritage left. Just think, if we fail to give emphasis to a moral climate, where will our democracy go? Some of us have been so busy looking after our own affairs that we have forgotten to look after the nation. Unless America recovers her rightful ideology nothing but chaos awaits us. Our destiny is to obey the guidance of God.

The true battle-line in the world today is not between class and class, not between race and race. The battle is between Christ and anti-Christ.

Choose ye this day whom ye will serve.

4

THE ANSWER TO ANY 'ISM' EVEN MATERIALISM

Address by Frank Buchman
Los Angeles, California, June 1948

Everywhere men long for peace and prepare for war. They long to rebuild and prepare to destroy. They plan for new prosperity and expect fresh disasters.

What is the missing factor in the planning and the statesmanship of the world today?

It is our lack of an ideology for democracy. We say, we are democrats, we need no ideology. We almost feel it is a sign of weakness to talk about an ideology.

So we try to meet the united plan and passion of alien ideologies with talk and with lip-service to high ideals and with a last resort to force. And we hope to live as we have always lived — selfishly, comfortably and undisturbed.

We have all lived too long in an atmosphere of imagining that security, prosperity, comfort and culture are natural to man.

We forgot the eternal struggle between Evil and Good, victory in which brings the blessings of security and prosperity. But defeat in this struggle, and even ignorance of it, brings proverty, hunger, slavery and death.

It takes more than diplomacy to exorcise evil. It takes more than lip-service to fight for God. Statesmen talk about the answer. They talk of union. But disunity increases. They talk of moral values. But immoral policies prevail. They use these words which the hard logic of events has proved true. But it remains words. These men do not face the cost in their own lives and the life of their nations of giving an answer.

An extreme of evil must be met with an extreme of good. A fanatical following of evil by a passionate pursuite of good.

That is why democracy fails. Only a passion can cure a passion. And only a superior world-arching ideology can cure a world divided by warring ideologies.

We Americans have been lulled into a false security by believing that all the 'isms' are across the sea.

'Isms' grow from unsolved problems in the life of men and nations. One man's hate kindles a million hates. One man's suspicion explodes a million suspicions. It spreads like a prairie fire. Or it creeps like a flame underground to burst out unexpectedly in a hundred places.

Is America free from hates, fears, suspicions, greed?

Why is our record of broken homes so high? How about industrial strife?

Are we victims of the greatest 'ism' of all? Materialism.

Is materialism the mother of all the 'isms'? Is materialism becoming our national ideology?

We stretch out generous hands to help Europe and Asia economically. But materialism frustrates our best intentions. Prices rise, money is worth less.

Troubles in industry cut down the supply of goods. At the moment when our strength is most needed abroad, we may find ourselves in our greatest crisis.

The other 'isms' are banking on that. They wait their time. They know that money, food, and clothes alone will not save Europe; that material things may make nations just strong enough materially to become their tools in their ideological conquest of the world.

Ten years ago Moral Re-Armament was born. In this very Hollywood Bowl the crowds gathered to see the preview of a new world order.

What have we learned in these ten years?

We have learned that democracy without an ideology can win a war but cannot build a peace; that ideological preparedness is the task of the whole nation, and is the one sure basis of national strength, moral, military and economic.

Today MRA offers the democracies and the whole world the superior armament of an ideology, without which armies are out-fought and statesmen are out-thought.

MRA has grown in ten years to the stature of a world answer to any 'ism' — even materialism. It has restored for millions the simple sanctities of home and honor, and given hope for a new world. It has built the world organism that can make a reality of this hope. In the words of a British coalminer, "Moral Re-Armament is the answer to every 'ism' even invented." It is for everyone everywhere.

Division is the mark of our age. Division in the heart. Division in the home. Division in industry. Division in the nation. Division between nations.

Union is our instant need.

Division is the work of human pride, hate, lust, fear, greed.

Division is the trademark of materialism.

Union is the grace of rebirth. We have lost the art of uniting because we have forgotten the secret of change and rebirth.

Moral Re-Armament is the good road of an ideology inspired by God upon which all can unite.

Catholic, Jew and Protestant, Hindu, Muslim, Buddhist and Confucianist — all find they can change, where needed, and travel along this good road together.

I called on a great leader in his time of deep sorrow. He gave me these words of Fulton Sheen, "What the world needs today is not to plead for religious unity so much as to plead for the unity of religious people." Those are the words of a great Catholic leader.

The Jew has his pristine contribution in the words of the great prophet-leader Isaiah, "Nations shall run unto thee because of the Lord thy God," and "Great shall be the peace of thy children." And in the words of the Psalmist, "Great peace have they which love Thy law; and nothing shall offend them."

And what does Islam say? The Foreign Minister of Pakistan, sent me this word, "Among my friends of MRA I have been delighted to observe the constant striving after discovering God's plan and purpose and putting their lives in accord with it. I am convinced that it is only through sincere and sustained effort in that direction that mankind can win through to its true redemption."

Is that the medium of approach for the Palestine problem?

It is so easy to have these great truths lost in prejudice. "Behold how these brethren fight one another," says the world. But it should be, "Behold how these brothers love one another."

Prejudice shall not keep any of us from the maximum leadership which our nations demand.

The Bishop of Tammerfors in Finland came to see that great ideological play *The Forgotten Factor* in his own land and language. He was afraid a play might not be the right medium. He came. He wept. He said, "This must go to everyone." After the first act he telephoned a well-known industrialist who came straight to the theater. As a result the cast was asked to show the play for a whole month.

What a joy must have possessed this Bishop who warily and almost against his will decided to come, and found the thing he most longed for for his nation — an over-arching ideology.

And what does India say? The Minister of Labor in Bombay Provincial Government, took this word back to the leaders of his country and to millions of India's workers, "Here is the force that can change selfishness and greed and all that is wrecking the spirit and soul of people. Until I met Moral Re-Armament I had not felt confident that there was an idea which could be applied universally as an adequate answer."

Now make no mistake. I do not say that this message will be wholly popular. It stirs the conscience. That is uncomfortable. It will always be open to misinterpretation by those who wish to escape it. But it comes as illumination to those who are ready.

Let me tell how it came to me. Just forty years ago I was divided. Just as nations today are divided. Materialism was winning its battle in my heart. I went to Europe to try to escape. But my battle came with me.

One day, in England, God showed me the cost of my pride and my materialism. I admitted it. That is the first step. Get honest.

I said, "Sorry" — first to God, then to those I had wronged. That is the second step.

I learned to listen to God. I accepted His commission to bring an answer to men and nations. That is the third step.

God is calling men everywhere to be the instruments of union. It comes not by conferences, not by laws, not by resolutions and pious hopes, but by change.

Change is the heart of the superior ideology.

As individuals change, a new climate comes to the nation's life. As leaders change, policies become inspired and the nation's life-blood flows again. As statesmen change, the fear of war and chaos will lift. The most difficult will respond to the firm, united but humble voice of reborn democracy.

Why should there be catastrophe again when, with God, renaissance is inevitable?

That is the new pattern of freedom for all nations. Shall it be a new Dark Age for Europe and the world? Or shall it be worldwide Renaissance of the moral and spiritual forces everywhere, bursting into life and bringing at the last moment a miracle to mankind?

Which shall it be? The decision lies in your hands.

5

TOMORROW'S AMERICAN

Address by Peter Howard
University of Southern California
Los Angeles, January 1964

I and my friends are out for a world revolution. Now revolution sometimes causes people to tremble. I don't mean a revolution of blood and force. I am out for a far greater revolution than that. I want a revolution rapid enough and radical enough to overtake and outstrip the astounding technological and industrial advance of our times.

Mr. Khrushchev, in Moscow, three months ago made a very startling statement. He said that after 46 years of socialist experiment, where environment had been used to the utmost to change the motive and character of man, he had failed to create a new type of man in the Soviet. Now, most people in my country just passed this by. Those who hate Communism hailed it as a great victory. Personally, I thought it showed a sign of hope. If you get men who for 46 years have relied on material things to create a new character in men, and have the courage to stand forward and say it has failed, I wonder what the free world can say to them. Or have we got to say to them, that in the lifetime of a man like Howard, out of the free world — the Christian world — in Europe have come two world wars, Fascism, Hitlerism and the social and economic injustice, the intolerance of class and color and race, that have provided the fuel of revolution in the Communist world?

Those things have got to change. Together we have got to create men free from hate, fear and selfishness — a type of man as different from the Stone Age man, the Steel Age man or the Dollar and Sex Age man as a spaceman is from a man pushing a wheelbarrow. That is our task. And make no mistake. If primitive man had not discovered the wheel, sophisticated man would not today be wheeling through space, and contemplating the colonization of the stars.

We need a revolution to carry the whole world forward fast to its next stage of human evolution — to outpace the growth of human power, wealth and skill with the growth in human character. If we succeed, we shall secure the peace and build a new world. We cannot do one without the other. There is nothing more futile, in my opinion, than those who talk passionately about peace and believe in peace and long for peace, but at the same time refuse to pay the price of building a new world fit for every man, woman and child to live in. We've got to undertake that supreme task together. If we fail, we shall enter a new dark age, or rather a new Red age, or we shall see man destroy himself with his own skill and the power and the problems he has created.

This revolution is one which all civilized people, certainly all people of faith, are called upon to undertake together. It is the most fascinating, most difficult and most demanding task of modern times.

I want to talk to you for a moment about freedom. It seems to me there are two immaturities at large in the world today. One is the immaturity of hate. America's strength is her heart-power. No nation in the whole of history has done what this nation has done for nations like mine. As long as men can think and read, your generosity and courage will be recorded. But your weakness is your hate-power.

I was talking the other day to a group of men who, I suppose, are among the cleverest men on this continent. Their brain far exceeds mine. When we got on to the question of civil rights, they rightly burned with indignation that in this country there still should be people who allow this deep division, this deep hatred, on account of the color of somebody else's skin.

But the very moment anybody rich was mentioned, anybody of privilege or background, those men blazed with hate themselves. They saw nothing inconsistent with hating somebody because of his background, but at the same time despising those who hated somebody else because of his color. Hate is hate, whether it is white against black, black against white, rich against poor, or poor against rich. And unless we find a fundamental answer to hatred, we shall not meet the challenge of this century.

Supposing America could really become, in the next five years, a country absolutely free of hate. Supposing this campus became absolutely free of hate — in the families, between the students, between the faculty and students — would you have something to say to the modern world? You'd have something to say that the United Nations have never yet said. You'd have something to say that the United Kingdom has never yet said. You'd have something to say that the U.S.S.R. has never yet said. And frankly, you'd have something to say that the U.S.A. has never yet said. But the whole world is waiting for it to be said.

The world is full of idealists who poison the atmosphere around them with hatred of somebody else because of their color, their race, their poverty, their wealth or their background. They are part of the problem whether they know it or not.

The other great immaturity is that of self-expression. It takes the form of doing what I like, when I like, regardless of what happens to my neighbor. Some people call it freedom. It is actually the inevitable death of freedom. It creates a belief that I'm basically a good chap, that my country is basically the best country, and that if only others understood what a good chap I am, and what a fine country mine is, everything would be in order. It is so soft, it is so stupid, but millions of dollars are squandered in the worship of this false idol year after year.

Some people say that people can't be changed. They say, "Why, the churches have been going for centuries and nothing much has happened." I was on a television program not long ago with a well-known European Catholic. A newspaperman was riding us quite hard on this subject. He turned to my friend and said, "You're a Catholic. Do you dare to suggest that the Church needs Moral Re-Armament?" My friend replied, "The Church doesn't, but Catholics do." And that is true, as a matter of fact, of all of us who profess a faith in God. We need to live what we profess, instead of camouflaging God by the way we live.

I first came across this work as a columnist who was paid one of the highest salaries in my country

for my exposés and investigations. I went cynical
—I had no faith at all. I had spent three years
studying philosophy at Oxford. It had the effect of
giving me a very sharp brain which I used to kill
my conscience. That is how I emerged from Oxford.
It also taught me how to earn a living, which I did
very successfully. It is a partial education, not a
whole education.

I went along to investigate Moral Re-Armament
and I straight away found people who seemed to
me to be adopting the most intelligent attitude to
modern events I had found. They said any idea that
keeps anybody out is too divisive and too dangerous
for the times we live in. Therefore, if you're going
to get everybody *in*, everybody has got to change.
And if you want to see history change, the most
practical place to start is with yourself and your
own nation.

Then they talked to me about absolute moral
standards. When they started talking about purity
and honesty and unselfishness and love, it didn't
take long for an Oxford philosopher to prove they
were wrong. So I instantly said, "Well, of course, all
standards are relative standards of behavior." And
a coal miner, well-trained in Marxism, said something I never forgot. He said, "If you have a standard at all, it must be absolute. Otherwise it is no
standard." I got cross because I knew it was true.
And in one simple sentence years of philosophic
training were swept aside. I was confronted with
reality.

Then I asked, "What do you really think?" They
said, "We think that people without faith can start
with absolute moral standards. That's the experimental method. Spend a few minutes facing absolute moral standards and see where you would have

175

to begin if you really wanted to remake the world. We believe that God has a plan for every man, woman and child in the world, and if you have faith, if you listen to Him, He'll tell you where to start." I said, "Don't give me that stuff because I don't believe in God." They said, "Well, that's fine. If you don't believe in God, you wouldn't mind making the experiment of listening to Him, would you?"

I could not object to that, although it made me feel squeamish, so I said, "Thank you very much," and went away. London had a heavy raid that night. I had certain duties to perform and was out all night. When I got home in the morning I thought, "Look here, this is either rubbish, or it's the most important thing you ever heard in your life. Have you got guts enough to try it?"

We British are very proud, and if anybody suggests we are too proud to make an honest experiment of that kind, sheer pride makes us try it. So I did. I got simple ideas. Pride can be useful at times. I got very simple ideas about honesty in the home. I had always wanted my children to be honest with me — my sons and my daughter — but I had never been honest with them. I had always wanted our government to be honest, but I wasn't honest about taxes. Quite simple things!

I longed to see a world truly united, but I only had one brother and I was jealous of him. I felt my parents liked him better than they liked me. Absolutely childish! There was I, a grown man, probably the most feared commentator in the country, jealous of my only brother. I had the idea that I ought to write and put it right. Do you know, three times I went down to that mail box in Fleet Street with a letter. Three times when I got there I tore it up. I said, "No!"

In the end, I wrote that letter. I just tell this somewhat personal story to show you the amazing things that happen if you obey. My brother came to see me. He was, of course, in the army, fighting. He gave me hell. He said, "I've always thought that about you. Now I know it's true." And he left. And I felt, "Well, there's not much in this." Two hours later he came back again, and he said, "Let's talk." We talked for the first time in years as brothers are meant to talk, with no shadows between us. We went to see my mother and father next day. The rift in our family was mended. That boy, because he was only a boy to me, found the beginnings of a faith in God. He was killed at Arnhem. And I had nearly been too proud to do the simple thing that helped him. Give him advice, sure! Give him money, yes! Give him a job, yes! Pat him on the back and say he was a great fellow, yes! But not do the one thing that actually helped him find a meaning and a purpose for his life.

One last story before I sit down. If you have a purpose and plan for humanity, backed with a discipline in your own life, you can tackle anybody. I am a very ordinary man. I've made more mistakes than most of you. I've been at it longer. But I was in Washington, D.C. not long since, at the Liberian Embassy. I was a guest of the Ambassador. I know the President of that country and hold him in high regard.

When I arrived, the only other white person there was a man a little younger than myself. He was very active, going to every single African in that place. I could see the man was working. He came up

177

to me. He thought I was a British diplomat. Some people would think that's a great compliment. Well, I endured it! He asked me where I had come from. It so happened I had come from Switzerland. He asked me if I knew any of the people negotiating about atomic disarmament, and I did. And then he said, "We in the Soviets have one great advantage over you in the West." I said, "What is it?" He said, "We have a strong ideology out to change the world, and you have a very weak ideology." I looked stupid — which I find quite easy — and said, "Do we have an ideology at all in the West?" He roared with laughter. He said, "Oh, you have no ideology at all in the West."

At that moment, by a stroke of ill fortune, the Ethiopian Ambassador approached, who happened to know me. He put out his hand and said, "Peter, what are you doing in Washington and how is Moral Re-Armament getting along?" Well, the Communists don't take a very good view of Moral Re-Armament. The Russians, of course, broadcast against us frequently on their national radio, and last year in 1963, Peking Radio broadcast to China that in their view, we of Moral Re-Armament were the only force that they still had to fear in the West. That is their view.

So this Russian at once turned to me and said, "You're against us." I said, "No, we're for you. We want to help you." "What do you mean?" he asked. I said, "The theory of the class struggle, carried to its logical conclusion, must result in atomic war between two great power groups. You know that." He said, "Have you read Karl Marx?" I said, "Yes, heavens alive, I plodded through him years ago and very dreary stuff he is, by the way." So then we got to talking dialectically.

The Russian said, "Of course, if you could change men, I should have to re-think the whole of my dialectic." I said, "You'd better re-think it."

I'll tell you two things that amuse me, because it shows where some of these men live. A girl came up while we were talking, and she offered us everything in the world you would want to smoke, from cigars — to — well, there was everything there, "reefers" as well, I expect. I didn't take any. So this Russian turned on me at once, with much scorn, because he was angry. He said, "Go on, have a smoke. Is there a rule against smoking in Moral Re-Armament?" I said, "No, there's no rule against smoking in Moral Re-Armament." He said, "Why don't you smoke then?" I said, "Every cent I have goes to my revolution and I wouldn't think of wasting a penny of it on tobacco." He said, "My God (God is the word he used), does it mean as much as that to you?" I said, "Why do you men think you're the only people who sacrifice for what you believe in? Do you think free men are incapable of accepting a discipline to further their cause?" He was shaken.

Then I told him that for years and years and years I and my friends had worked without salary; that actually the royalties from my books and plays, amounting to £400,000 sterling, have all been given to the work of Moral Re-Armament before publication. It happens to be my contribution to the work.

He took me out in the garden. He was really hooked by now. He took me to the bar. He thought he had got me nicely. He said, "Come on, have a drink. They won't charge you anything." I said, "No, thank you very much." He said, "Is there a rule against drinking in Moral Re-Armament?" I said, "No." He said, "Why won't you drink then?" I said,

"I will," and took a Coca-Cola. He laughed and said, "What's the reason?" I said, "When I'm with a man like you I prefer to keep my head clear."

But it wasn't the whole truth. I'll tell you, as we're friends here, why I don't drink. There is no rule about it, but I get people from all walks of life who come to me with problems, some of them with habits they cannot break. And I know in my own life that if I am in the grip of any habit, I cannot help them. That's why I don't drink. But as far as you are concerned, drink just as much as you feel will help your neighbor. That's the way I feel about it. That's fair enough, isn't it? That's good Americanism.

I just want to say this, and I want to say it because our own future in Britain, of course, depends on you. Our past depended on you — you came to our rescue in the war. Western Europe owes its liberty to you. The African countries owe their liberty to you. Asia owes its liberty to you. The whole future depends on which way America goes now.

America is the most wealthy, powerful nation of our time, or of any time in human history. There has never been a nation so wealthy and powerful. She is a generous, brave, inventive, childish giant. I don't think America understands the world she lives in. I don't think she understands Communism, and I don't think she possesses the answer to it. I think she is against it. That's a different story. I believe America thinks Communism is the sharing of wealth and that free enterprise is the reply. Now, don't get me wrong. I am all for free enterprise, but it has little appeal to thin men who possess nothing. Have you ever thought of that? If you are an Asian or an African, with too little to eat, and no hope of getting

180

much tomorrow, talk of free enterprise has no great appeal.

In any case, Communism is far more than making thin men fat, or fat men thin. And that is about the level at which some people put it in this country. Communism is a bid to alter the character of humanity. It is a ruthless determination to achieve that end, defiantly demonstrating that man is nothing but water, chemicals, gas and dust, assembled by accident, conditioned by environment and dispersed into oblivion as the brief light of day fades and night falls.

Lenin said, "We shall never succeed until the myth of God is removed from the mind of man." He also said, "Our morality is wholly subordinate to the interests of the class struggle." That means what suits us is right, and no free nation which adopts that same morality — what suits us is right — has any answer to the challenge of world Communism.

Communism is the worship of materialism — the worship of rubles or dollars, the worship of human flesh and human brain, the worship of success or recognition, the worship of heroes whether they are dressed up as dictators or presidents. It is putting man first. Communism is the denial of God. It condones the immorality that springs, and springs only, from a disbelief in Him.

The answer to Communism is not merely anti-Communism. Hitler was the greatest anti-Communist that ever lived. Have you ever thought of that? He succeeded in spreading Communism across half the globe and killing himself in the process.

Men who speak against Communism, but have hatred in their hearts against members of their own family, their fellow students, or members of the faculty, against people of another class, race or color, are in fact spreading the Communism they denounce and deny. A free-for-all society, money-minded, sex-centered, success-driven, may strengthen but will never answer Stalinism or Hitlerism, for it is the hotbed of materialism where dictatorship breeds and democracy dies.

One nation God-centered — or if you don't believe in God, a nation centered on the morality and spirit and character of men — teaching men to accept absolute values of honesty, purity, unselfishness and love, and to obey that inner voice which distinguishes all men from any beast. Such a nation will lead mankind forward beyond known frontiers into the new territory of lasting human freedom. I believe our task is to bind up the wounds of centuries and to set all continents free. And with all my heart I believe America can do it.

6

WHAT COLOR IS GOD'S SKIN?

Address by Peter Howard,
Wheat Street Baptist Church,
Atlanta, Georgia, February 1964

One hundred years ago and more, President Lincoln signed his proclamation of emancipation. It was a revolutionary aim. Today our aim is more revolutionary and more far-reaching in fulfilment. It is a revolution for every red-blooded American. And I must remind you that every American's blood is red. It is and ever will be the greatest revolution of all time whereby the Cross of Christ will transform the modern world.

Some people are afraid of the word "revolution." No man of faith should be. "Thy kingdom come. Thy will be done on earth as it is in Heaven." If that phrase becomes no longer a pious drone but a passionate commitment, it is more revolutionary than any Fascist state or than anything Karl Marx concocted. It affects all we say, do, think and are. It involves race, class, color, personality and nationhood.

In new patterns of power unfolding across every continent, revolution to change the aim and character of humanity is blazing in urgency. Let us ensure that blaze creates more light and less heat.

Otherwise the world may be lost in darkness. Man with his mind has wrenched secrets from earth and atom that can in his generation give all men everywhere food to eat, homes wherein to dwell, a fair chance and proper background in life. He has with his skill plunged like Leviathan beneath Arctic ice caps and ridden with Mercury among the stars. Man's hands control strength to populate new planets or destroy this one with the problems he has created. His heart still lingers in the dust and debris of senile, sterile prejudice, outworn attitudes, pride and selfishness that have crumbled and failed.

Too many still walk the earth who are too fat, too many who are far too thin. There is enough for everyone's need, but not for everyone's greed. But man does not yet care enough and share enough so everybody has enough. At a time when it is God's will and man's desiring for everybody — black, brown, white, yellow and red — to walk with head upheld in dignity, equality and peace, selfishness alone breaks homes, divides races, multiplies hate, bedevils the hope of a moral maturity to match the technological and industrial opportunity of our times.

The different races in America are her strength and glory. They can be her supersonic missile of revolution in the modern world. They are no handicap. They are an asset that no other country possesses.

In my lifetime, whole countries have been taken over by the cruel dictatorship of Fascism and countless millions are now controlled by the godless philosophy of Communism. To our shame, not one city, not one state, can boast that it is controlled by the living God.

Supposing America, with her Negro and Latin

184

American and Caucasian and Indian minorities, were able to proclaim in honesty to the listening earth: "Come and see how all men everywhere are meant to live. We need you all in our bid to change world history, which is the destiny of our age. In this dangerous, essential task, black men, white men, all men are needed. Here in this land we live like sons and daughters of the God who created all men equal, planting in each human heart the knowledge of right and wrong that makes man different from a beast."

Africa, emerging into freedom, would leap with joy and clasp hands across the ocean. Asia would turn her eyes to the West. Latin America would forget the flirtation of Fidel Castro and follow the advances of her comrade in the North.

This brings me to a question no man can answer. What color is God's skin? In fifty years, if things continue as they are, half the population of the earth will be Chinese. The South African Government seems to think the Chinese are black. Contrariwise, because South Africa does much trade with Japan, the same Government says Japanese are white.

Laws are important. Laws are essential. I am one who believes that legislation must often march or even run ahead of the growth in man's character which makes much legislation unnecessary. But laws — though in South Africa they change the color of a human skin — cannot by themselves alter the character of a human heart.

On the day President Kennedy was assassinated, I talked with two American Negroes. They spoke of civil rights. They agreed that a civil rights bill with teeth would probably pass through Congress. Then one said: "Whatever laws pass Congress, I can never trust a white man. It is in my bones to hate them all." Unless you have been a white man, you don't know what it means to have that said to you.

Englishmen like myself were taught from our mothers' knee to believe that because we were white and English we were better than everybody else. It breeds the immaturity of that effortless superiority, often unconscious, always so cruel, that millions across the face of the earth have experienced and resented. We do not look down on people because they have a different colored skin. We just feel nicely sorry for all those who are not born English.

I told those American Negroes how I, an ordinary Englishman, had made the experiment of listening to the voice of God, the inner voice that speaks to each human heart. I had seen that it was the selfishness, arrogance and pride of men like myself which had caused untold misery, suffering and injustice.

When I spoke to the men and women of the Mau Mau, detained in the Athi River Camp in Kenya, they covered their faces as I drew near. They would not look at a white man. My first words were: "I was born white. I could not help it, could I?" They began to look at me. It began to slide upon their understanding that it was as immature and ignorant to hate a man because he was born white, as to hate him because he was born black, brilliant, foolish, ugly, beautiful, big, small, Jew or Arab. When I had finished speaking, their leaders came to me and said: "We were educated in Christian schools. We lost our faith and became cynical of everything except violence to achieve liberty because of the way we saw white Christians live. We want you to know that if we had dreamed white men could speak and think as we heard you speak today, there would have been no Mau Mau in Kenya."

> *When I survey the wondrous Cross,*
> *On which the Prince of Glory died,*
> *My richest gain I count but loss*
> *And pour contempt on all my pride.*

I felt in my heart the shame and agony of the words these Kenyans spoke to me. I wept. Some of these former Mau Mau leaders have become my friends. They saw white men change. They learned that black men, too, could change. They changed. They now are on the march with people of all colors and races to bring God's revolution to the continent of Africa. They understand that violence, sometimes regarded as a good servant, can swiftly become a bad master, and that history never long remains on the side of hate. Hate knows no color bar. Neither does love. Heart power is America's strength. Hate power is her weakness.

The two American Negroes said to me: "Do you think education and environment can change human nature?" I long for every man, woman and child to have the best education and environment civilization can provide, but neither environment nor education changed me. God did. My wife, not English, but married to me for thirty-one years, says: "Moral Re-Armament changes everybody — even the English. And if that can happen, there's hope for the whole world."

Everybody wants to see the other fellow, the other class, the other race, the other nation change. Everybody is waiting for the other to begin. Modern Fascists and reactionaries are those who want things different but are unwilling to be different themselves. Modern pioneers and revolutionaries are those who are so impatient with things as they are, so passionate for things as they must be, that they pay the price in their own lives of the change they wish to see in others. A hate-filled man will never unite a society or even a family. Men driven by greed, pride, or fear will never build justice, liberty or lasting peace.

The white man's world is ebbing. For a long time the white man has been in a minority on the face of the earth. By accident of history, by design of power, white men have controlled much of the planet. That time is swiftly ending. Communications, education, automation — all will combine to shift the power balance of humanity.

God made men in different colors. A white man's world, in the sense that a white man, because of the color of his skin, is closer to God than is his neighbor, affronts the will of the Almighty and the understanding and conscience of humanity. So does a black man's world. So does a world of yellow or red domination. We need a world where all men walk the earth with the dignity of brotherhood that should be normal to all who accept the fatherhood of God.

The Negro is neither worse nor better than his neighbor. The same is true of the white man. We all have our loftier side, and our more debased. There are two sides to each coin — heads and tails. In the West there has been too much tail, too little head. And the heart, which could and should be the leaven of society, lies forgotten between pride of intellect and lust of desire. We exploit our wife or somebody else's wife, our neighbor, our business rival, and scream out against exploitation.

America will set the continents free when she experiences lasting freedom in her own heart — freedom from the immaturity of hate, the under-development of selfishness, and the infantility of impurity and dirt.

I number many Africans among my friends. Not long ago, I traveled with some of them in this country. It is strange that in communities where the white American will no longer listen to the Negro, and the Negro will no longer listen to the white American, both will heed the voice of Africa. These Africans were invited to the homes of Southerners, white and black. Some of them, people of prominence and distinction in their own countries, stayed in the homes of American Negroes. At the end of a few days, they came to me and said: "Some of them treat us in the same way that they say some white men treat them. The same superiority, the same condescension, the same contempt."

We white men are prone to tell everybody else how to live and what to do. But we are too proud to listen to the voice of God, and ourselves, in obedience, learn how to live. We preach unity with passion and call ourselves the United Kingdom or the United States. We transfer idealism to the United Nations but we remain, behind the doors of our homes, our offices, our churches, deeply divided from each other — by jealousy, ambition, greed or prejudice. I pray the black man does not fall into the white man's ways in this regard.

Today, the long-awaited tide of history flows towards the non-white races. Those tides will lift burdens of the centuries and wipe out bloodstains in the sands of time. Be sure that tide elevates all humanity. You cannot expect every Negro, any more than you can expect every white man, to be a genius of ability, a paragon of virtue, a miracle of grace. But I hope, pray and expect that the Negro people of the United States will have the wisdom, understanding and human greatness to avoid mistakes that men like myself have made before them.

There was once a great Baptist preacher called Spurgeon. Multitudes came to sit at his feet. One day he said: "We Baptists can proudly make our boast: We never persecuted those who differed from us on religious grounds." When the "Amens" and "Hallelujahs" died away, Spurgeon added: "We never had the chance."

The black man's chance is surely coming. What will he do with it? I do not say: "Be patient." I say: "Be passionate for something far bigger than color. Be passionate for an answer big enough to include everybody, powerful enough to satisfy the longings for bread, work and the hope of a new world that lie in the heart of the teeming millions of the earth."

Segregation yesterday. Confrontation today. Transformation tomorrow. Let the hands of the black man stretch out above the heads of governments and nationalities to embrace and welcome all people who are ready with them to remake the modern world.

Unless we accept a world aim, we may be lost in narrow disputations. It is difficult, if not impossible, for others to place confidence in a system of democracy that preaches inalienable rights of the individual with its lips, but robs men of their rights with its customs. Yet it is true that nothing would suit the enemies of freedom and of America more than to see this country tear itself apart with its internal wars, preoccupying itself with mutual strife, while dictatorship takes over the rest of the world. Some demagogues, enemies of liberty, white and black, inside and outside America, desire to push the problem for the sake of personal power instead of curing it for the sake of all the people.

It is a paradox of our times that Communism, which says it believes only in materialism, bids powerfully for the mind and spirit of humanity. Democracy, which declares its faith that man has the spirit of God, the Holy Spirit within him, bids for the allegiance of humanity with materialistic aid, but without a revolutionary aim for the whole world.

Lenin said: "Our revolution will never succeed until the myth of God is removed from the mind of man." In free society we print on our money, "In God We Trust." But if in truth we place the claims of cash, comfort and color before God, we justify with our lives the theories of Marx no matter what we say with our lips.

It remains my firm belief that crossless Christians have done, and still do, more to camouflage from humanity the reality of Christ's revolution than any Communist or Fascist.

There are sincere men in the free world who have no faith in God. To them it can be said: "Then accept the challenge of living in the way you would wish to see your neighbor live." Absolute moral standards of honesty, purity, unselfishness and love are a yardstick by which all men can measure their conduct and see where change is needed. If you have a standard at all, it must be absolute. Otherwise, it is no standard. And those four standards may prove a ladder that leads a man towards faith.

We say God is love. It is fair to add that throughout history many who professed a faith in God have hated their neighbor. My wife gave me one of the best definitions of love I have ever known. When first I accepted the challenge of this revolution I went to her and was as honest with her as I had always wished our children to be with us. She said to me: "Peter, I think I am meant to love you as you are, but to fight for you to become the man you are meant to be."

This I believe is true love, where black loves white, white loves black, all Americans love America, and America loves the modern world enough to live so that black, white and the whole of this torn and suffering earth become as they are meant to be in the mind of the Almighty.

My faith is in modern America. I believe Americans will arise and shine forth with a character that convicts, captivates and changes nation after nation. I believe that those who have suffered most will show the greatest passion and compassion for long-suffering humanity. I believe that those who have been victims of the worst discrimination will be the first to heal the hates and fears of others because they themselves are free from fear and hate. I am convinced that men and women who for generations have drunk the water of tears and eaten the bread of bitterness, will give living water and the bread of life to millions — trembling, longing, hoping, waiting, praying, for the new type of man and the new type of society that will lead the world into lasting justice, liberty and peace.

Those who have passed through the fires of persecution can hold forth one hand to persecutors and persecuted alike, and with the other uplift a flame of freedom to illuminate the earth.

7

MODERN PAUL REVERES

Address by Peter Howard
Mackinac Island Michigan, August 1964

I want to thank every single one of the delegates to this Assembly. When we started, I said that age had much to learn from youth. Only the most stubborn, selfish, senile could have lived through this Assembly and not learned great lessons in life from young people who have been here. Perhaps many of you have things to learn. But those of us older people who have not had some great, growing experiences of God have missed the miracle.

I don't go for this talk of leaving. It's for the grasshoppers. We never need leave each other. We are bound by the steel bands of a common revolutionary task. Anybody who wants to leave can leave, but the rest of us can stick together as one force in a growing world family "till kingdom come."

There was a man called Paul Revere and he rode, and in spirit certain people rode with him. The great majority did not. Some of them never left their wives, their beds, their comforts and their corn. Some turned back. But the people who built the nation and who are remembered by history were the men who rode. And you are going out today like so many Paul Reveres.

Don't be a bit disconcerted if not everybody rides with you. They won't. Don't be a bit disconcerted if some people get the collywobbles when the bullets fly. They will. But the people who ride and keep on riding are going to make a permanent mark on the history of this country and on the story of liberty.

Since George Washington I don't know when any group of Americans have set forth to serve this country, determined to finance their revolution on their knees. It's extremely healthy and you're going to do it.

If I had medals for you all, I'd give every one of you a medal. I don't have medals. And I don't think you would want them if I had. But you're going to the places where you could earn them.

I hope you will run into the heaviest kind of artillery. If you find artillery firing, you know you're on target. And don't be confused by it one bit. If you live in West Virginia, which is a glorious place, and if you heave a rock out of the window and a dog starts howling, you can be sure you've hit something. And if I were you, I'd just keep on heaving the rocks.

You've all got plans, haven't you? Does the United States of America have plans? Do all the plans of the United States of America work? Why not? I won't puzzle you. This is not a contest morning. Of course, the plans are enormously important, and your imagination and dare can shift this country. But no plan will ever work unless it is backed by convinced, disciplined people. And that is what impresses me so much about most of you. You have caught the vision of a revolutionized America and a revolutionized world. You are ready to back it with the discipline of your lives. That is what counts.

You ought to be so different when you go back

home that your own dog, if you have a dog, bites you. A lot of you are. But some of you are not. I say to those who have just a few more hours of battle preparation before you go where the bullets fly: big doors swing on little hinges. Remember that. Sometimes the hinge on which a big door swings is just about the size of a cigarette, sometimes it may be a relationship, sometimes a habit. Sometimes that hinge is just that 5 or 10 percent that we still hang onto.

I'll say one thing from my own knowledge. If you have a 5 or 10 percent which you still hang onto, that is what runs your life. The thing we hang onto and will not give is the thing that runs us.

We have had very clear diagnosis in this assembly of the world situation. But some people diagnose for years and they never bring a cure. There was a man I was fond of when I worked in newspapers. And the comradeship of the press is one of the finest kinds of comradeship on earth outside of Moral Re-Armament. I was devoted to this man and we spent ten years diagnosing him. It's what some people do for the troubles of America or the free world.

This man's problem was very simple. He was a Christian and he drank too much. He was too fond of women. He spent money he hadn't got and his home was hell. I tried to help him. I used to give him money because I had a lot in those days. I used to give him one drink about six o'clock at night and then bring him back into the office. Of course, as soon as I'd said goodbye, he'd go out and have six more drinks.

Diagnosis, perfect. We all knew his problems. Nobody brought a cure.

The very day that I attended to the hinges in my own life on which big doors swung — they were quite simple, paying back money I'd stolen, getting straight with my wife and children, facing my arrogance as an Englishman — that man came up to me in the office and said, "I want to talk to you, something has happened to you." He changed. He went back to his church. He got straight about money. And until he died, he was a much loved father and husband.

Diagnosis is one thing, but building an answer that works is another. And a faith to take that answer to the nation is another still. Let anybody criticize Moral Re-Armament who has himself built a force like this to carry an answer to America. If they have done it, let them speak. If they have not done it, let them learn. That's fair enough, isn't it?

The real links — the bridge — between emotion and action are concrete, costly, daily decisions. People who refuse to change will accuse you of emotionalism and a million other things. Don't be fooled by it one minute. It only means that you've got your drill right on the nerve. So keep on drilling. Watch them jump and howl and soon they'll change.

I think we have an answer here. I want to tell you the verdict of two men.

The newspaperman Al Kuettner, head of the Southern civil rights desk of United Press International, has been twice praised, once in *Time* magazine and once in *Newsweek*, as one of the greatest American reporters covering the racial situation. He came up here to Mackinac. He'd just been in Mississippi. He'd just been in Florida. He was sick at heart because he is a decent American. He said at the end of three days, "You have here the answer the whole of America is longing for. And nobody else is giving it to us."

Then there was the actor Sidney Poitier. I quote

to you what he said on the telephone from Hollywood two days ago. "I cannot get out of my mind," he said, "that you have the living demonstration America is seeking." That man cares very deeply for humanity.

One thing which I know impressed him, and which has enormously impressed me, is these Indians. That Indian play yesterday troubled me deeply. I'm glad I have been invited to New Mexico. And I want to say again that the Indian people can live and give something to every section of America and the world which no other people can give. There are certain things the white people can do, certain things the colored people can do, but the Indians can speak with absolute authority to both, and they can speak to the world with a voice that has not yet been heard from America. Think how the Asians will listen to you. Think how the Africans will listen to you. Think how the Latin Americans will listen to you. And they're going to listen if you do your job when you get home.

I want to say one last thing, and it is about Communism. A lot of people talk about Communism. But the point statesmen in my country, and I think in America, completely fail to grasp, is this: Every trained Marxist dialectician knows that according to his own belief, either freedom is going to be destroyed, or Marxism is going to be destroyed, or eventually they'll destroy each other.

So, in the mind of a convinced Communist there can be no permanent accord between his idea, and the ideas of liberty and God. In the free world we so hunger for peace that we are willing to come to terms with anybody provided they leave us alone. That's why today Russian socialism is the modern version of that famous agrarian reform movement in China. Do you remember? There was no Communism in China, it was just a great, big agrarian reform. I think the theory started in Britain. You don't like British cooking in America, with some reason, but you sure do swallow British philosophy. And then that great agrarian reformer, Castro, the hero of the peasants, do you remember him? You even unbelted 7 million of your big, capitalist New York dollars to finance Castro — and he skinned you alive.

You had Castro agrarian reform, you had Chinese agrarian reform. Now, heaven help us, you've got Russian socialism as the answer to Chinese Communism. And America is pushing that down the throat of Asia. She's pushing it down the throat of Africa. She's pushing it down the throat of Europe.

Do watch it, because if those are facts, and I believe them to be facts, and if Lenin meant what he said, "We can never succeed until the myth of God is removed from the mind of man," then the only intelligent action for the men who love liberty is to create a revolution bigger than Communism that needs everybody to carry it forward. Then you can say to the Communists, "We want to revolutionize the world. We are going to revolutionize the world. Come and help us do it in the right way."

That is the only synthesis that will get the Marxist out of his dilemma. The Communists know it. That's why Moscow frequently recognizes Moral Re-Armament as the ideology of democracy in the modern world. That is why Peking attacks us so ferociously and says we are the only people they fear. Sooner or later, democracy too will recognize this truth or perish. It could happen both ways — recognition of an answer or destruction from lack of it — sooner

Frank Buchman (right) visited Mahatma Gandhi in his Ashram in 1924. They first met in 1915. Gandhi called MRA "the greatest thing that has come out of the West."

In 1938 Carl Hambro, President of the League of Nations Assembly, asked Buchman to bring MRA force to Geneva. "Where we have failed in changing politics," he said, "you have succeeded in changing men."

30,000 people crowded Hollywood Bowl for meeting in July 1939 which launched MRA on the West Coast.

Philip Murray, President of the United Steelworkers and the CIO, speaks after showing of "You Can Defend America" at union's 1942 Convention in Cleveland.

Buchman with Ray F. Purdy, MRA pioneer, and Admiral Byrd the polar explorer, in Washington, 1946.

French Foreign Minister Schuman and Dr. Buchman at Caux, Switzerland, September 1953. "International conferences," said Schuman in addressing the MRA Assembly, "normally end with great disappointments. Here we find a great hope."

German Chancellor Adenauer and Buchman in Los Angeles, January 1960. Adenauer wrote later in the press, "Dr. Buchman is making a great contribution to international unity and the establishment of social justice."

Niro Hoshijima (left), veteran Japanese Diet Member who accompanied MRA Statesmen's Mission to Manila, June 1955, apologized publicly for Japan's war-time actions and was warmly received by Philippine President Magsaysay (right).

Shah of Iran sees command performance of "Vanishing Island" in palace grounds, Teheran, August 1955.

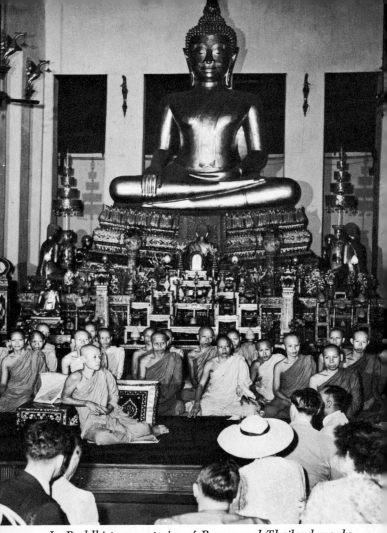

In Buddhist monasteries of Burma and Thailand monks welcomed MRA Mission in 1955–56 and several of their leaders visited Mackinac and Caux. Said the President of Supreme Buddhist Councils "The ability of MRA to change man is proof it has power to unite the world."

"Atlanta will never be the same again," said Judge A. T. Walden, speaking in Washington, after a performance of "The Crowning Experience," which ran many weeks in Atlanta at a time of racial tension in 1958.

Japanese students, whose Tokyo riots prevented Eisenhower visit in June 1960, apologize to Presidential Press Secretary James Hagerty after performance of their play "The Tiger" in Carnegie Hall, N.Y., 1961.

An estimated 40,000 Peruvian Indians perch on rocks around Sacsayhuaman Fortress above Cuzco to see "The Tiger" given in the Quechua language in October 1961.

Former Prime Minister Kishi of Japan describes 1961 visit to MRA assembly at Caux, Switzerland, as "the most significant twenty-four hours of my life."

Sparked by "The Tiger," revolutionary Latin American students wrote a play "El Condor" in 1961 "to answer violence and corruption." They took it through the Americas and Europe, then filmed it to reach millions.

In October 1963 in Trivandrum, South India, 100,000 lined streets to watch start of 3,400-mile march led by Rajmohan Gandhi through 29 cities to New Delhi to rouse India to a revolution of national character.

Peter Howard, British author, playwright, athlete, farmer and MRA pioneer until his death in February, 1965. In his last visits to America he stirred a generation of youth to take on new goals for the world.

Representatives of 48 Indian tribes of North America were hosts to Demonstration for Modernizing America at Mackinac Island, Michigan, June, 1965.

At opening of the MRA inspired Mackinac College, September 1966, were President Cornell (left), Catholic Bishop Noa of Marquette, Michigan and Episcopal Bishop Selway of Northern Michigan.

BOARD OF DIRECTORS

MORAL RE-ARMAMENT, INC.

J. Blanton Belk
Executive Director

H. Kenaston Twitchell, Jr.
Secretary

Donald P. Birdsall
Treasurer

Paul S. Campbell, M.D.

Basil R. Entwistle

William T. Close, M.D.

Robert H. Hogan

George L. Eastman

Stewart V. Lancaster

James E. MacLennan

Wm. Van Dusen Wishard

William F. Wilkes

John C. Wood

Eugene J. von Teuber

T. Guy Woolford

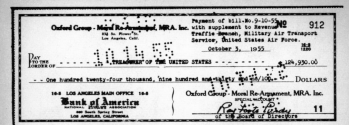

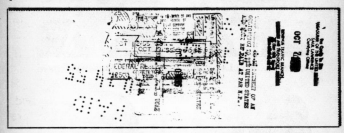

Facsimile of check with which Moral Re-Armament paid for Air Force transportation for the Statesmen's Mission.

Title page of Gestapo Report on the Oxford Group (MRA), ordering its suppression wherever found by the armed forces of Nazi Germany.

than we think, because history is marching at a prodigious pace.

In the next months you in the United States have got to match the revolutionary passion and relentlessness of men determined to take over Latin America, take over Africa, take over Asia — and who are not, repeat not, going to leave this country and Canada to stew in their own juice.

If you interpret this as an attack on Communists, you're wrong. I think Communists for the most part are wholly sincere in their desire to revolutionize the world. What I hate is the self-righteous condescension of men and women in the free world who say they believe in God, but live as if He never existed, and think we can continue our selfish, comfortable, easy-going, divided ways undisturbed. That is modern madness. And I believe you are going out to end it.

8

THE COMING REVOLUTION

Address by Peter Howard
The Foreign Office, Rio de Janeiro, Brazil,
January 21 1965

I was once paid a high compliment. It came from a Russian who met me at a reception in the Finnish Embassay in Washington, D.C. He mistook me for a diplomat. It was, of course, a mistake, but it is one of my treasured memories. I am no diplomat. I, therefore, propose to tell you in straight terms what I feel. If, because of my lack of experience in the arts of the world where you gentlemen live and move, I say anything which breaks diplomatic rules, forgive me. But it is better to be understood than to strive merely for appreciation.

We are living in an age such as man has never known. Man's brain and hands have created more produce and wealth than ever before. In the midst of it all, millions go to bed hungry and awake without hope. And the human family is increasing in numbers as the sands of the sea. Man holds power to destroy all life upon the planet. At this very moment, millions turn for leadership to those who are not only unafraid of violence, but seek it as a means to achieve their goal.

In the opinion of Mao Tse-tung, China has less

to lose from nuclear warfare than most countries. A few days ago a letter appeared in the London *Times*. The letter described how Mr. Nehru of India, shortly before he died, revealed that Mao Tse-tung, when talking to him in Peking, said that China alone of the nations of the world could well afford to suffer two to three hundred million casualties and so had least reason to fear a nuclear war. This so horrified the man to whom Nehru told this tale that he asked, "Did Mao Tse-tung really say that?" Mr. Nehru gave the assurance that he had. Mr. Nehru was a truthful man.

Last year, Chou En-lai told some ambassadors in Peking, "War is not only inevitable but necessary to achieve world Communism. In such a war, I would be ready to loose 300 million lives." Two months ago he was reported as saying that he would be ready to destroy half of humanity if he could build socialism in the half that remained. This is Communism's answer to the social and economic injustices and sufferings that cover large areas of the earth. Many sane people would regard a program which envisages the destruction of half the world as a program that had already failed. But, of course, the Communists regard man as nothing more than an animal wearing clothes, lipstick and shoe leather. Beria, formerly head of the Russian Secret Police described man in the following terms:

"Man is an animal. He is an animal which has been given a civilized veneer. Man is a collective animal grouped together for his own protection before threat of his environment. Those who so group and control him must then have in their possession specialized techniques to direct the vagaries and energies of the animal man towards greater

efficiency in the accomplishment of the goals of the State."

In other words, the State can use slaughterhouse, torture chamber, lash and whip to control the zoo over which it presides.

I am bound to say that I do not regard this attitude as more wrong than the attitude of nations which proclaim a faith and call themselves Christians, but who tolerate gross corruption in matters of tax and industry, who allow the rich to grow fat from the leanness of the poor and who, while crying the name of God aloud, abandon moral standards and live in impurity and indulgence exactly as if they were the animals the Communists declare them to be.

The most dramatic failure of the Communist world is the split between Russia and China. Personally, I do not rejoice in this split. Any deep division in the human family is fraught with peril for us all. Some people say that Communism has become a mere instrument of nationalistic policy in the hands of power-hungry men. This may be true of some Communists. I believe it is false about the vast majority of them. Communism, whether you agree with it or not, is passionately resolved to change the world radically and rapidly. Millions go to Communism because they see in its program the only hope of something new for themselves and for their children.

Some other people say privately that it is now necessary for the United States to form an alliance with Soviet Russia in order to contain, or even to crush, China. I am reminded of the time before the last World War when certain influential people in Britain decided that it would be excellent to come to terms with Russia in order to crush Hitler. They forgot that Russia also had to agree to this arrangement. For months the British negotiators waited in Moscow. Then, like a crack of Red lightning, came the news that Molotov had signed a treaty with Ribbentrop. Germany and Russia proceeded to destroy and devour the carcass of Poland. Stalin supplied Hitler with food and equipment in his efforts to conquer my country. It is hard to criticize the Russians for hoping Germany and Britain would grind each other to the grave and leave them in peace, when that is precisely what some of us in Britain had hoped the Germans and Russians would do to each other.

America has tried to answer the determination of Communism to win the world. She has been more generous in her dollar aid than any other nation in the whole human story. She is stronger in arms than any other nation. Her system of education is the best, the comfort of her environment is the highest in the world. She has cultivated an attitude of anti-Communism in her policies at home and abroad. But, in spite of this, Communism is still there, and in continents like Africa and Asia, Communism strides forward. Wealth, strength, anti-Communism are not enough. If they were, America would have swept back the Red tide long since.

In Western Europe at the end of World War II, the Communist Parties were strong. They had been a mainspring of resistance to Hitler. They were led, for the most part, by highly sincere and intelligent people. But in Western Europe, Communism has, if anything, retreated. The reason is simple. In Europe some of the great post-war leaders understood the need for ideology to answer ideology. They believed that an ideology of freedom was necessary if free men were to show the Communists that their philosophy was wrong and that there was more in a man than liquids, muscles, fats and bones that would all turn to dust in due season.

The Americans poured money into Europe. They poured arms into Europe. By their policies they built NATO as a political and military shield. But no great idea came from America to Europe that could include everybody — Communist and non-Communist alike — in the supreme purpose of putting right what was wrong throughout the continent.

Three men — Adenauer, Schuman and de Gasperi — from three different nations — Germany, France, Italy — decided to stand together to build Europe. Those men were united in their political philosophy by being pupils of Don Sturzo. They were helped to this effective action by their conviction about Moral Re-Armament. Schuman would have retreated into private life in 1949 but for a conversation with Dr. Buchman, initiator of Moral Re-Armament. Instead he took up the task he most feared — that of reconciliation with Germany — and for which he faced bitter criticism from his own people. Adenauer knew the part played by Moral Re-Armament in the creation of the economic unity of Europe. When the Schuman Plan agreement was signed he said, "Moral Re-Armament played an unseen but effective part in bridging differences of opinion between the negotiating parties in recent important international agreements." De Gasperi echoed this in his conviction that MRA went "to the root of the world's evils and will bring about the understanding between men and nations for which all people long."

Robert Schuman wrote, "If Moral Re-Armament were just another theory, I should not be interested. But it is a philosophy of life applied in action, which

I have seen reaching millions. It is a world-wide transformation of human society which has already begun."

Don Sturzo, who had trained these three great Europeans, described Moral Re-Armament as "fire from heaven" before he died. And two years ago Adenauer told the press, "Unless Moral Re-Armament is extended, peace cannot be preserved." Of course Adenauer, Schuman and de Gasperi all happen to be Catholics. They all knew perfectly well that Moral Re-Armament was no substitute for the Church. They knew this was not a new sect — a Protestant sect or a substitute for any church. They knew, as Schuman described it, that it was a philosophy of life applied in action, reaching the millions.

Here was the foundation of post-war Europe. If Europe is in difficulties today, it is not for lack of money and prosperity or of powerful weapons. It is because Europeans stopped short in building the unity of Europe. They were content with too small a goal. They did not realize that the only answer to revolution on a world scale is a greater revolution, which also must involve the whole world. Some of the European leaders realized this truth but many lacked the will to act together, to surrender personal ambition and indulgence, to out-sacrifice, out-challenge and out-work those who want to maintain a divided world today in order to profit from it tomorrow.

There is another attitude in the free world towards Communism which must be marked. Powerful men say privately to each other, "Communism is inevitable. We had better quietly let it come and hope that in God's good time, quietly it will go." One of the best-known and most influential diplomats of the Western world spoke to a friend of mine who had been banished from a position of leadership in an Iron Curtain country. He told him last year in Geneva, "Communism is inevitable. The task of free statesmen is to see that it wins the world without a war. It will last probably for a hundred years. In the end it will purify the churches, which may be a good thing for everybody."

In the same way in America today you get voices like that of Senator Fulbright — whose integrity cannot be questioned but whose comprehension anyone in a world still free is entitled to doubt — reported by *The New York Times* as saying that moral absolutism must be abandoned and that in effect the ends justify the means. Of course, he may have been misreported. But if reported correctly, this is precisely the Communist case, and is bound to help appeasers in America and elsewhere who want to see Communism, under the title of "agrarian reform" or "Russian Socialism" or "a popular front" establish its control of continents. This appeasement is a policy fraught with grave danger. I will tell you why.

Hitler was fooled by the horror of the ordinary men and women of my country and other countries at the prospect of war. He believed that if he went on pushing long enough every gate would fall before him. He discovered too late that there comes a point beyond which you cannot push men of faith who love freedom. If they have to choose between submission or death, they choose death. Today, Germany divided and a great wall built through the heart of that country are memorials to his folly. These modern appeasers of Communism do not understand that there comes a point where men will revolt. America will never, as a nation, be bullied or pushed into the Communist camp. Sooner than submit she will drop her bombs. Therefore, in an atomic age, those who hope to avoid total destruction by undercover submission on a world scale in effect bring world war nearer every day.

Brazil is a sign of the times for those with eyes to see and ears to hear. The Brazilian revolution was not, in fact, a revolution by one class or in the interests of one section of the nation. It began out of the revulsion of millions of Brazilian women against the corruption and trend of the times. It was revolt by Brazilians for Brazil. But the revolution has only just begun. The test of it is yet to come. It will be whether Brazil can demonstrate to the whole world that free men can fill empty stomachs with food, fill empty hands with work, and fill empty hearts with a passion to remake the world more efficiently, more swiftly and more justly than any Fascist or Communist regime.

One test will be whether inflation is conquered. It can be. But it will take remedies that hurt. It is vitally important that this country can never be accused either by its own people or by foreigners of taxing the little men but letting the big men go free; of being more energetic about putting down Communism than in ending the corruption which is a cause of Communism. A start of greatest importance has already been made. It was told yesterday that for the first time it is becoming dangerous to be dishonest. Some big tycoons are faced with the threat of big penalties for big corruption. Thank God some men have been given power to act who believe that those who will not sacrifice their selfishness for their nation will be prevented by tough measures from sacrificing the nation for their selfishness and greed. The test is whether leaders will lead, employers will create employment, and workers will work. Leaders who do not lead and employers who do not create employment are as responsible for inflation as workers who will not work. And no big sacrifice will be offered by the ordinary man unless leaders offer him, too, a big aim which he can understand and love.

I do not mean in this speech to express my judgment as to whether Communism, as millions say, is the remedy for human ills, or whether Communism, as other millions say, is the disease of our times. The one thing I do know is that Communism is a world issue. It cannot be dealt with locally or nationally. People who think they will answer Communism by putting Communists in gaol in this country or that, are like men who think they will cure a patient suffering from measles by painting out four square inches of the spots. Why is it that Communism has people in every part of the world who, of their own accord, help its cause forward; whereas the democracies are so concerned with their own concerns that they will not even stand and help each other in a continent like Latin America or Africa or Asia? It is simply because Communism, whether you regard it as good or bad, has a world aim which its adherents pursue with passion, philosophy and plan. Its world aim comes first, and the life of every Communist is submitted to that aim. It is called ideology.

Why should free men or men of faith, who deny the Communists' charge that they are mere cattle, accept a lesser aim for their lives, pursued with lesser discipline and lesser sacrifice than those who follow the doctrines of Karl Marx? There is an alternative to the acceptance of appeasement of

Communism or atomic war against Communism. It is a world rebuilt. It is a revolution big enough to include non-Communist and Communist alike, and powerful enough to change the materialism in both, which is the root of the human problem and which remains long after tyrants are slain, or those who want to subvert a nation are gaoled. We can never rebuild the world unless all nations, all races, all classes, all colors are included in that essential and urgent task.

We need in this age of astonishing human achievements in technology and science and force, the astonishment of a new aim in which all men can share. That is the creation of a new type of human society, built by a new type of man. Khrushchev, just before he fell from power, stretched out in mind towards it when he admitted that forty-six years of socialist experiment in the Soviets had failed to create a man free from hate, or fear, or greed. The free world condemns itself if, with all its material advantages and its belief in a Supreme Being, it continues to live with the appetites, cruelties, divisions and fears that man knew when he lived in the caves.

Moral Re-Armament is an ideology of freedom for all men everywhere. Whether the Communist or the non-Communist world needs it most, God alone can decide. Certainly, if both accept their need, we shall see an age of sanity, justice and lasting peace. One nation demonstrating the speed with which men can learn new and greater aims — without which they will plunge into the old wars that will lead this time to the everlasting silence — could give hope and challenge to Moscow and Peking as well as Washington, Paris and London. Such a land could be Brazil. You have the chance.

Nobody suggests the present Government is corrupt. Most people declare it is the best Government this country has had for many years. Everybody knows the nation is waiting for the next forward step of the march you began here last April. Perhaps the men and women in the favelas, the workers in the docks, the craftsmen in the fields and mills will shake off inflation with a burst of triumphant energy if they are told that Brazil is going to lead the world through Moral Re-Armament in a new direction. It will mean change for the Government and change for the governed, change for the rich who can afford it better than the poor, who also need it. Here would be a Christian nation showing the world that God, for the first time this century, was becoming relevant and powerful in the family life, industrial life and international policies of a great nation. Free nations committed to Moral Re-Armament as fully as Russia and China are committed to Communism would pioneer the next step of progress for Communist and non-Communist blocs alike.

Frank Buchman gave his last words to the world, "I want to see nations governed by men governed by God. Why not let God run the whole world?" This may not be diplomatic language. It remains the only diplomacy that will work.

9

WILL YOU TACKLE WHAT NEEDS TO BE DONE?

Address by J. Blanton Belk,
Estes Park, Colorado, June 1966

You have come from all over America. I salute you and your delegations for the way you have sacrificed and raised your money to come here to Estes Park.

I, like you, have the highest hopes for what is going to come from this "Action Now Demonstration" in the Rockies of Colorado. I think I have come the farthest to be here. Ten days ago I started out for Estes Park with my wife and Mr. Birdsall. Lenin used to say the shortest route to Washington was through Peking and Calcutta. I can tell you honestly, the shortest route to Estes Park is through Bonn, Bombay, Bangkok, Hong Kong, Tokyo and Hawaii.

You and I have hope for Estes Park, but I tell you seriously, the world's eyes and hopes are on young America and what you will explode from this Demonstration for a generation around the globe. In Asia, Europe, Africa and South America they have glimpsed your Sing-Outs and they know in nine short months what young Americans, through Moral Re-Armament, have inspired and set in motion in the youth of the world.

The Sing-Out story is already a legend in its time. We thank God for the military, economic, scientific, technological, monetary might of America. But in the midst of this young America has exploded, through a living demonstration, an idea from the heart of the land that can yet bind up the world's wounds and set nations free. In this secular age a dynamic new faith has burst forth from young America and gone out to the world.

Here is a generation that will not be blackmailed by the secular, satanic, sensory view of some parts of our society who say that human nature cannot change, that man is the highest authority, that right and wrong are old-fashioned, that God is dead, that nothing new can happen that has not already happened.

But neither is this a generation that takes for granted anything because somebody says so. It is a scientific age and you are a scientific, experimenting generation. You will try, and decide for yourselves.

That is what Sing-Out is — a generation experimenting and exploding with an idea that has been valid for them and they believe for their generation. It is not an idea they are demonstrating in America and abroad to Americanize people or control people, but to revolutionize and release all people from their small aims and purposes that have divided and held humanity back.

"Up, Up With People" is their theme song.

A generation is ready to march with this idea. Peter Howard saw this clearly. In one of his last plays *Through the Garden Wall*, it was the young people who, because the wall never existed in their minds, walked through it constantly. It is a generation with no barriers, no divisions of color, class, nationality, religion, background, who are bursting to build something new. For a better description, they are a true "internationale."

Time is not on your side in this revolution. Only the speed, pace, guts, dynamism, militancy and all-outness, that is latent in your generation, if mobilized to a white-hot pitch can alter the world picture in time.

You must not waste one more hour of your life on earth in feverish activity, or just activity. That is not the way, nor relevant to the world scene. Protesting, hating, bitterness, phony patriots who say you have to criticize your country to be a patriot, will never carry the world forward.

The idea that captures your generation will capture the world.

All of us know that half the population of the world is under 25. Take Mexico. Half their population is under 18. Brazil the same. Japan; half the population under 20. Africa. In most of the new cabinets the average age is under 30. Half the population of Russia is under 26. And those under 12 years of age in China outnumber our total population in America.

At a moment when many people say that Communism and capitalism are growing more and more like each other, the youth in Russia are saying, "Give us something to believe in." Mao Tsetung is saying, "What we lack is a revolutionary morality for our youth."

Nations in Africa as well as Asia are looking to see if we have something new to offer from America. I just heard from Rajmohan Gandhi that the intellectuals from all over India for the first time have turned away from Russia and are taking a fresh look at America.

There is an interlude at the moment when something new could emerge everywhere in the world.

Take Europe. Old alliances are crumbling, such as NATO. Old enemies like Germany have suddenly become our best friends and old allies like France we find ourselves divided from.

It is easy to wipe off General de Gaulle by saying that he is an obstructionist. It is childish to suppose that a man of de Gaulle's experience, wisdom and patriotism would not have some reason for what he is doing. He deeply believes that national traits and national pride are stronger than any ideologies that may come and go. He thinks his nationalism can win and woo the countries in the East such as Rumania and Poland, and unite with Russia. Right or wrong, de Gaulle loves his country dearly and believes in her destiny.

Former Chancellor Adenauer, who, I suppose, knows de Gaulle as well as any man, said to me recently that General de Gaulle is not anti-this country though sometimes he has been handled the wrong way. What he is looking for is something brand new coming out of America. So far he has not seen it; but if young Americans could demonstrate this idea of Moral Re-Armament to de Gaulle, it could be a new bridge between America and France.

The important thing is that we Americans do not close our hearts and minds to France but probe for a way to build this new bridge. Maybe it will come from the youth. The French are concerned about their youth. Last year they spent $30 million in an effort to find an adequate program for them.

Then you have the Russian Foreign Minister, Gromyko, misusing his visit with the Pope to call for a summit conference in Europe without America. He proposes a return to the Rapacki Plan, which would mean the neutralization of Europe with Germany as a nuclear-free zone. It all adds up to a strong bid to have America withdraw her troops from Europe.

Unfortunately, we have certain men in America who echo the convictions of these men. But Dr. Adenauer also said to me, "Europe may become America's Achilles' heel unless you find a world commitment for the youth of America."

And today American youth are explosively seizing that world commitment and the youth of the world are responding. At a time when the war in South Vietnam is being used to divide the world from America, 150 young Americans — Negro, white and Indian — in "Sing-Out '66" have been in both Asia and Europe giving such an image of a new America that everywhere people say, "If this is America, we are all for it."

Mr. McNamara has said the youth of the whole country should do some form of national service. But Sing-Out has been demonstrating this national service all this past year in every sector of national life. And you have shown that youth on their own will choose to serve if the purpose and aim is big enough. Mr. McNamara also spoke of the need for new ways of building bridges to nations that have cut themselves off. This, too, must be done and you have demonstrated how it can be done in Asia, Africa and Latin America.

The other night when I was in Bombay and meeting the youth in "India, Arise!" the first thing they said at the end of the show was, "We have been waiting to meet you so we could ask you, 'How do you multiply?'" Because they have the passion to multiply themselves fast enough to be in time.

Moral Re-Armament was not given to the world to be a palliative, nor to provide a modern catacomb for a few while mankind goes on a jungle march of self-destruction. Moral Re-Armament is an idea that was given man to be in time, to salvage man from himself and enable him to undertake his creative mission here on earth.

There is urgency in Moral Re-Armament. The job must be done now, with the speed of revolution, with all the skills and facilities of science and technology. Many will have to turn from personal careers to national commitment. And many who would like to carry MRA as their good work will have to turn to carrying world revolution, and to mobilizing their nations as vehicles for such revolution.

I think our next great wave forward in the world is going to be in education, a radically new type of education. It is fifty years behind the times. It is no longer exciting. It is not creating history. It cultivates spectatorism and noninvolvement. But the youth in Sing-Out have been learning history. Seventy-three students have taken correspondence studies with the two traveling Sing-Outs this winter. Some of the youth in the high schools on the road with Sing-Out were not students to begin with. One of them told me: "I was an 'F' student. Now I am a 'B' student because a purpose has come into my life." He has found a new red-hot reason for learning.

Then there is Mackinac College launching out. It is not going to be what you think of as a college. It is going to be the most exciting, creative, new kind of academic training America has ever seen. It will be dynamic and it will propel you into action now. There will be a different element in this college.

Adenauer said of it, "Thank God someone is going to train young Americans in foreign affairs." Some of you in the college may have a semester or two in the college and then the next semester you may be in a language school in Europe preparing for your chosen career. Or you may be on the road with your professors in Latin America or Africa putting into action the knowledge of the lecture halls.

What will be tapped is the creative potential of this generation. High grades will not be the only test of entrance or continuance in this college, but also the ability to grapple with the facts of life and to lead men and to lead nations.

The college will generate a new breed of leaders, men who have the ability to inspire people to new motivations and train people to world aims. It will be like a War College for man's creative mission here on earth. It will combine theory and practice to produce men who have the guts and experience to carry out what needs to be done in nations today.

Recently I had a letter from the publisher of a large newspaper chain who wrote: "Many thanks for sending me a copy of your PACE magazine. It is excellently done with a very modern touch, both as to subject matter and execution. The reason I can state this so authoritatively is because my 16-year-old son thought it was 'better than LIFE.' You are, of course, on the right track in appealing to the youth of today in their own language and on subjects which are of great interest to them . . . P.S. . . . Can you please send me another copy because my son took mine."

A corporate executive said to me the other day: "The two magazines bidding for the youth today are *Playboy* and PACE."

America has the money and the means to do now what needs to be done. And you youth may be the key to getting it. You may not have brought that much money with you to Estes Park, but I will tell you frankly that if you decide to sacrifice and pay the price without remuneration to secure freedom for your generation and those to follow, you can ask industry and government to help you, and keep on asking them until the job is done, and they will give you the finances.

You are offering to President Johnson, to Vice President Humphrey, to Dean Rusk, a committed trained force of young Americans that can carry forward with realism, urgency and creative speed these great aims for America and the world. Here are young men and women prepared to see the job through. We are not going to pull back or pull out, at home or abroad.

Today I ask you: Will you be the rock for the nation on which all the tides of little men with little or no aims will break? Will you be that rock? Your generation could be the steel girder that would hold the world together.

You will have a million new ideas and fresh concepts as you pick up this task and commit yourselves to it.

Three men have meant a great deal to me as I have committed my life to this battle.

My father introduced me to Moral Re-Armament and taught me that faith must be militant, fighting and all-out or it is not a faith. I remember riding along with my father as a small boy and passing a long freight train with a beautiful red caboose at the end. My father turned to me and said, "What would you like to be, the engine or the caboose?" I answered immediately, "The caboose." My father

It is a battle that deals with life here and now.

The millions must carry the world forward to the dynamic freedom of nations governed by men who are governed by God. God's control of a nation is not only possible; it is lunacy in an atomic world to think in any other terms.

Through no special virtue of our own we have become the wealthiest and mightiest nation of the 20th century. We rightly decided that as a people we cannot live in easy isolation enjoying our own freedom and prosperity. We have to discover how to share them with the whole globe. This is the supreme task of the last half of the 20th century. It is not easy.

It was one thing in '76 to take freedom into our own hands and develop a continent of free people. But in '67 it is a far bigger job to bring the machinery of prosperity to the millions of mankind and do it in the framework of freedom for the heart and spirit of man.

In case you don't know it, this is what America has set her hand to and we can be glad and proud that she has.

People ask: "Why did we ever get into Vietnam?" Because the Vietnamese people were in desperate need for help, simple economic help, and no one was prepared to supply it. America responded to that need.

It has turned out to be a far bigger job than we first imagined and goes far deeper than sharing wealth. It confronts us with the basic issue before the western world: Can free men create a new society; or must we leave it to the Communists?

I don't believe we need to. I believe that the whole American people need to become involved in Vietnam. They need to be adult about the world now. It is not good enough to send our youth there as a military shield, and withhold our own hearts and wills from the task of creating a new order of society. There needs to come to the millions a down-to-earth commitment to America's world calling. The youth of "Up With People" are the vanguard of this nation's purpose.

What is lacking in America is the popular will to carry that purpose. If we have the will we shall find the way. We are a privileged people to be given this task by history. We will let humanity down if, through selfish aims and complacent living, we refuse the job before us. Complacency breeds confusion and we fall prey to points of view about policies at home and abroad pushed on us by self-assured opinion-makers in press and TV.

Take the draft. A great froth is whipped up in press and political circles about the draft, yet it is obvious horse sense. If a free people are to carry a great task in a dangerous world, they need an adequate military arm. Why shouldn't it be a matter of pride to serve whether you fire a musket or sew a flag?

There is a further value to our present-day military training. I quote William R. Matthews, one of our most seasoned editors in the nation's press: "I made an official investigation of the Navy, Air Force and Marine Corps recruiting camps in San Diego. I was dumbfounded with satisfaction and surprise at this wonderful training, which turned youngsters into self-reliant men. It brought out their best qualities by the education, clean living and discipline that is still imposed on them."

In today's military training youth grow up fast. An enlisted Marine told me how impressed he was with the swift entry into self-reliant manhood of the trainees around him. I wish every young American could have the chance with the military or with Moral Re-Armament to give at least two years to the service of his country. Universal national service of that kind would unite the growth in character and the multiplication in manhood that are demanded of America's youth today.

If this over-riding commitment became the climate of our family life, America's homes would become the revolutionary cells of her purpose and aim in the world.

The poverty of purpose in American homes has been the parent of the rebellion of the youth and the proliferation of divorce. It has made America known around the world as a nation of broken homes.

Tackle this poverty and you will create families who advance the nation to great purpose. They will become the revolutionary frontline of America. They will demonstrate the answer to the destructive violence of the young Red Guards in China.

We need to tackle the universities and colleges of America. No country has put more of its money, public and private, into higher education than has ours. We have created the finest facilities, and set up flourishing faculties. We have institutions whose stored wisdom, knowledge and techniques should be pouring out a tide of mature leadership to serve the nation's needs at home and abroad.

But we are getting a crop of unkempt, undisciplined, irresolute youth whose chief concern is no bigger than themselves, and who become the pawns of a loud-mouthed minority.

Unless we learn to use our universities in the

right way, there are those ready and scheming to use them as engines of class war, race war, and social and moral collapse.

You can supply our university youth with the incentives and pattern of dedication which will make our universities the most effective engines of Moral Re-Armament, nationally and worldwide. Out of them should flow the creative genius of a generation with a plan for humanity.

During these days in Santa Fe we have been planning specifically and practically what we are going to do in the next two years.

What will you have in mind for the Pacific basin? For Europe? For Africa? For North and South America?

You will have to live globally and learn to assess the world, not by press columnists and TV commentators, but by the moral realities which have become the North Star of your lives.

Will you join "Sing-Out Germany" in Brazil and move with them in Latin America?

Will you join with Japan's Asian Sing-Out and move through the Pacific?

Will you with the Indians of North America take this answer to the 70 million Indians of the Western Hemisphere? Will you with them become the shaping force that you are meant to be in the world?

Will you saturate the universities of America with a stature and purpose worthy of our age?

Will you this spring draw together the youth of the world into a giant "Up With People" Festival, and demonstrate to the nations the will of the oncoming generation?

Will you and your parents stir adult and senior

America out of apathy into active involvement in your aims for the country?

Will you make a firm bid to government, to industry, press and TV to get behind you and launch you nationwide and worldwide?

It is going to take a lot of cold hard cash. Your phenomenal advance this past year has used up every cent that has come to us. We have come to this conference very much in need. We are grateful to the homes and citizens of Santa Fe who have taken us in and given us the facilities in which to meet.

For one thing, PACE magazine needs expansion funds of a million dollars to lift it into the national orbit it merits.

Mackinac College must have two million to see her through the year's building program and the operating costs of its initial year.

Your "Up With People" program will have to expand. You will need further national casts. You will have to operate as America's most effective "people-to-people" ambassadors in other continents. You will need all of seven million to carry these things forward.

You merit massive support and enlistment. This last year you have demonstrated the basic answer to the problems that concern our nation at home and abroad. You have the right to ask for what you need, and America, I believe, will gladly give it to you. What you ask is very little compared to the millions America is pouring into programs of welfare and enlightenment that are vitally needed but require your MRA factor to become effective.

You saturated one town with "Up With People" a year ago. The Chief of Police reports a 70% decline of delinquency in the schools since then.

Last winter the man in charge of one of the Government's Job Programs in Michigan came to inspect the building operation on Mackinac Island. He had heard its volunteer crew came from the same background as the men he was trying to employ.

When he left he said: "You have the answer to the Poverty Program. Our crisis is with the man who comes to us, learns what to do, gets started, then bang, he hits the bottle and goes delinquent. At this point you step in, change the man and he becomes an effective worker."

In Puerto Rico, after the first night in San Juan a truculent youth approached one of the young men in the show, socked him in the eye and fled. The next night the same Puerto Rican came back and made his way to the young man he had socked the night before. The cast member who is a hefty youth squared away to even the score. The Puerto Rican quickly held up his hands and said, "Don't hit me. I came back to apologize. I was wrong. I've joined the local Sing-Out."

A thousand Puerto Rican youth are developing Sing-Outs all across the Island.

In Jamaica, at the Kingston premiere of Sing-Out, everyone expected the violent youth from the slums to sally forth and sabotage the show. They did sally forth, but they carried placards welcoming the Sing-Out youth from America. A new wind is blowing through the Caribbean.

A year ago our President said to the nation: "I am going to ask you for more discipline." He hit a keynote that millions responded to.

There is something in America that does not want a soft job or small one. She is ready to respond to a great task, provided it is big enough.

What is the President going to ask of us in the year ahead? Will it be a task of leadership that matches the might of America?

In Europe they ask: "Is America withdrawing from Europe to help Asia?" In the Pacific they wonder: "Is America so preoccupied elsewhere that she will cut short her commitment here?"

Let us make unequivocally clear from the youth of America that she is not going to withdraw from any friends, old or new. But she is resolutely fixed to stand forever firm with all who love freedom all around the globe.

PACE PUBLICATIONS

835 SOUTH FLOWER STREET
LOS ANGELES, CALIFORNIA